# Don't Text Them!
*How to Heal and Move On from Toxic Relationships*

### Olivia Johnson

Copyright © 2022 Olivia Johnson

All rights reserved.

ISBN: 9798368186306

# ACKNOWLEDGMENTS

### © Copyright 2022 - All rights reserved.

The content contained within this book may not be reproduced, duplicated or transmitted without direct written permission from the author or the publisher.

Under no circumstances will any blame or legal responsibility be held against the publisher, or author, for any damages, reparation, or monetary loss due to the information contained within this book, either directly or indirectly.

Legal Notice:

This book is copyright protected. It is only for personal use. You cannot amend, distribute, sell, use, quote or paraphrase any part, or the content within this book, without the consent of the author or publisher.

Disclaimer Notice:

Please note the information contained within this document is for educational and entertainment purposes only. All effort has been executed to present accurate, up to date, reliable, complete information. No warranties of any kind are declared or implied. Readers acknowledge that the author is not engaged in the rendering of legal, financial, medical or professional advice. The content within this book has been derived from various sources. Please consult a licensed professional before attempting any techniques outlined in this book.

By reading this document, the reader agrees that under no circumstances is the author responsible for any losses, direct or indirect, that are incurred as a result of the use of the information contained within this document, including, but not limited to, errors, omissions, or inaccuracies.

# CONTENTS

|   | Introduction | 5 |
|---|---|---|
| 1 | Red Flag Alert | 9 |
| 2 | Rope Burn | 29 |
| 3 | At Arm's Length | 49 |
| 4 | Time to Detox | 67 |
| 5 | Oops. I Did It Again | 79 |
| 6 | Raising the Bar | 87 |
| 7 | Back and Better | 97 |
|   | Conclusion | 105 |
|   | *References* | 109 |

# Introduction

Have you ever been in a relationship that began as a whirlwind romance, only to wake up one day to have the butterflies in your stomach replaced with a sinking feeling that you are being ignored, intimidated, and constantly drained by your partner? Or perhaps you have a sibling who is manipulative and deceitful towards you, who causes conflict for no reason? Has your friend suddenly turned their back on you without warning, giving you the cold shoulder and silent treatment? Does your manager bully, falsely accuse you, or undermine your work performance solely to make you feel small?

If you answered "yes" to even one of the above questions, chances are that the relationship you find yourself in is toxic. A toxic relationship can be personal or professional, whether between a spouse, romantic partner, family member, friend, boss, or colleague. The signs are often invisible, and thus unintentionally overlooked by people on the outside. This tends to create feelings of helplessness, confusion, desperation, despair, and loneliness in those of us who are directly involved, creating emotional trauma that can have long-lasting mental and physical effects. Relationships are the foundations of our interactions with others. Recent evidence suggests how damaging toxic relationships are not only to the individual but to society as a whole.

This book is designed to help you recognize and recover from toxic relationships by recommending useful strategies to heal and form healthier connections. Written from experience, and drawing on extensive research that relies on reputable, credible, and reliable sources, the aim of this book is to educate, enlighten, and encourage anyone, from the age of 16 to adulthood, who seeks support that, in many cases, is not available elsewhere.

Some of the questions this book addresses are these:
1. How do I know if I am in a toxic relationship?
2. How can I get out–and stay out–of an unhealthy relationship?
3. Am I able to survive this relationship and will I ever feel whole again?

In the following pages, you will find realistic and reassuring advice on how to break free and remain distant from controlling, verbally abusive, and emotionally manipulative people. Here you will discover how to identify a toxic relationship and why setting boundaries is important for your health and happiness.

Some of the most vital things you will learn in this book are how to

- love yourself enough to know that you are worthy of better treatment.

- remind yourself that you do not deserve the pain and trauma of an unhealthy relationship.
- not to be afraid to let go of someone who is toxic to pursue your best interest. Yes, you will survive without them!
- not beat yourself up when you make a mistake and fall back into the same cycle. It will be hard, but you can and you will overcome it!
- not be ashamed to ask for help from people you know have your best interests at heart.

The most important thing to remember here is that many others share the same painful experiences. You are not alone. No one deserves to feel less than worthy, especially because of someone else's actions.

## Chapter 1: Red Flag Alert

**You're Probably Surrounded**

We have all encountered that person who is miserable and draining to be around, the "wet blanket" who sees life as a glass half empty and brings others down with negative and judgemental comments. There's also that person who has a large group of friends and gets along with everyone, the "life of the party," who quietly makes comments that make you question yourself. Toxic people surround us, permeating our homes, social circles and workplaces. They can easily enter our lives, often slipping in quietly through the cracks without our realization. Learning how to identify the red flags of toxic behavior is imperative in safeguarding yourself from the potential harm such people can cause.

In her book *Toxic People*, Dr. Lillian Glass—an American interpersonal communication expert and body language specialist—defines a toxic person as anyone "who is not supportive, who is not happy to see you grow, to see you succeed, who does not wish you well. In essence, he or she sabotages your efforts to lead a happy and productive life" (Glass, 1995, p.12). Dr. Glass extends her definition to define a toxic relationship as one that is unbalanced instead of harmonious, while being a constant source of conflict, where one person disrespects, does not support, and continuously criticizes the other person.

Data analysts Nazaria Solferino and Maria Elisebetta Tessitore define a toxic relationship as a "relationship disorder characterized by a disparity, with an unequal hierarchy in which one person becomes dependent on the other, triggering a mechanism of dominance and subjection" (Solferino & Tessitore, 2021, p.3). In April 2020, as Covid-19 lockdown conditions became the "new normal," *The New York Times* reported a sudden increase in emotionally abusive relationships worldwide as people were forced to spend more time in each other's personal space (Taub, 2020). This indicated that being surrounded by "toxic people" is slowly becoming the "new normal" of relationships.

Over the past few decades, the phenomenon of emotional abuse and its effects on interpersonal relationships has become of particular interest in the field of psychology. Author of multiple self-help books on the subject, Beverly Engel, describes emotional abuse as "any nonphysical behavior that is designed to control, intimidate, subjugate, demean, punish or isolate another person" (Engel, 2002, p. 12). Studies are increasingly indicating that emotional abuse is more prevalent in relationships than physical abuse. However, emotional abuse is much harder to detect, often remaining unnoticed or misunderstood by those not directly affected. This kind of unseen abuse is thus much more difficult to address, and ultimately remedy, which often leaves those who are on the receiving end to suffer in silence.

*Note to reader:* I purposefully refrain from using the word 'victim' here because of the negative connotations the term carries, that are the exact opposite of the hopeful and non judgemental messages emphasized in this book. Instead, I describe toxic behavior as potentially far-reaching and long-term effects on the recipient's health. The impacts on mental health include depression, anxiety, self-doubt, lack of confidence, reduced self-esteem, confusion, an impaired ability to think logically or make rational decisions, feelings of helplessness, despair, anxiety, regarding oneself as unworthy or unloveable, and ultimately a depreciation in personal value and a lost sense of self. In addition, several studies have pointed out that being in a toxic relationship could impact physical health in various ways, such as causing high blood pressure, heart problems, insomnia, chronic fatigue, and/or extreme weight loss or gain (Karakurt & Soliver, 2013; Pai, 2018).

It's important to know that toxic relationships can be abusive, but not all toxic relationships involve abuse. In an article written by Cindy Lamonthe, a journalist focused on the science of human behavior, she explains the difference between toxicity and abuse as the unintentional versus the intentional. In many unhealthy relationships, one or both people may exhibit toxic traits and not realize it; while still hurtful and harmful, neither party intends to abuse the other. Toxicity turns to abuse when a person exercises power over the other with intentions to control their behavior and cause harm. (Lamonthe, 2022). Due to the amount of toxic relationships, it is likely that everyone has experienced a toxic person in one form or another, and it is likely that you have exhibited toxic behaviors as well. According to Solferino and Tessitore's article "Human Nextworks and Toxic Relationships," approximately one in three women and one in four men experience physical violence in their relationships (Solferino & Tessitore, 2019).

The goal of the knowledge you will gain throughout this novel is to become aware of red flags, or signs of toxicity in interactions whether stemming from yourself or others, and to take action to correct your behavior or set boundaries to protect yourself from someone else's.

Toxic behaviors in unhealthy and sometimes abusive relationships can include one or a combination of the following: gaslighting, manipulation, narcissism, lying, selfishness, arrogance, bullying, etc. These behaviors are not specific to romantic relationships and can be seen in family dynamics, friendships, and relationships at work and school. If you have watched TV shows like *Inventing Anna*, *Gilmore Girls*, *The Office*, *Gossip Girl*, or *Friends* you've seen fictional depictions of toxicity. Something to ask yourself and to consider about your social relationships is whether or not you, or that person, are contributing to the dynamic or detracting from it (Everly, 2019).

*Gaslighting*

Gaslighting causes the recipient to question their feelings, instincts, and, ultimately, their reality. This is when someone refuses to acknowledge their role by insisting that something didn't happen, that they didn't say or intend to say what you have brought up, or they may turn the tables and tell you that you have anger issues, that you are incapable of trust, or perhaps that you are a pessimist who needs to look on the bright side and stop being so dramatic (Lamonthe, 2022).

One example of gaslighting in a fictional relationship is between Ross and Rachel on the TV show, *Friends*. The famous "were they/weren't they on a break" dilemma is a prime example of gaslighting. Ross diminishes and dismisses Rachel's feelings and perspective by taking the focus off of his hurtful actions during their time apart and putting it on Rachel, insisting that she's being dramatic and remembers their conversation incorrectly, rather than admitting to his hurtful actions and having a conversation about what had happened and how they can move forward in their relationship. In this case, Ross is being the toxic person, but there are many instances throughout the show where they both exhibit toxic traits.

This can happen in a friendship as well, like in the show, *Inventing Anna*, where Anna Delvy deceives all of her friends through gaslighting and manipulating them into believing that her struggles trump theirs. She uses deception to make them feel guilt and pity toward her, and ultimately gaslights them into giving her time, money, and material possessions to bring her out of her state of crisis. This type of gaslighting, based on true events, is an example of emotional abuse as Ms. Delvy knew exactly what she was doing, that it hurt people and put them in a state of confusion, and, despite this knowledge, intended on climbing the proverbial social ladder by any means necessary.

## *Manipulation*

While gaslighting is about gaining control over another person and is a kind of psychological manipulation, manipulation itself is about getting our own way by beating the "system." The two behaviors can go hand-in-hand as Ms. Delvy shows in the way she used people to gain wealth, move around the world, and gain a highly credible social status all through the elaborate lies she told to get ahead. Everyone goes through tough times and needs support; however, a toxic person may use their struggle to manipulate you into doing things for them or spending time with them. Of course, you'd want to be there for a friend or family member in their time of need; however, if you have expressed not having the mental capacity or the time to help in their moment of perceived desperation and they turn to criticizing your friendship, this would be an example of manipulation (Lamonthe, 2022).

Another TV show that consistently represents toxic behavior like manipulation is *Gossip Girl*. If you've watched this show, you may have noticed the dynamic between Blair and Serena, and likely other characters as well. They often manipulate the truth or come up with lies that will only benefit themselves. Similarly, Chuck and Blair often manipulate each other to get what they want. Chuck knows Blair so well that he can use his knowledge of her personality against herself and make her do things that she would otherwise refrain from. In the popular show, *Saved by the Bell*, Zack Morris gaslights Kelly Kapowski multiple times by convincing her that the seemingly dumb things he does that hurt her are actually very romantic and ways he shows his love. This makes Kelly question her feelings in situations with Zack and with other people in her life as well as distorts the very premise of what love is supposed to feel like. Love doesn't hurt or confuse you, love is supposed to feel easy and natural (Merinuk, 2022).

### *Narcissism*

Much like the terms above, this word is being thrown around in social circles and online communities amongst people who have gone through a recent breakup. Medical editors at the Mayo Clinic, a non-profit organization with focus on medical research and education, define narcissism as "a mental condition in which people have an inflated sense of their own importance, a deep need for excessive attention and admiration, troubled relationships, and a lack of empathy for others" (Mayo Clinic, 2017).

These types of people tend to be charming in the beginning and often look for friendships and partners in people with low self-esteem and people who look up to them. People with low self-esteem are sometimes attracted to narcissists because they can be viewed as protectors. However, a narcissistic person feels like rules don't apply to them unless they benefit from them in some way; therefore, these relationships turn toxic rather quickly. When confronted, a narcissist will not accept blame, will deny claims of aggression; instead, explaining it as being assertive, and will result in gaslighting and manipulation to confirm their inflated sense of self (Everly, 2019).

A narcissist may be obvious in some situations like Miranda Priesly in *The Devil Wears Prada*, who puts appearance above all and shows a lack of empathy or compassion toward her employees, offering a high-level job and more responsibility to a new employee instead of the one who had been loyal and committed for years. Or they may be harder to spot like Carrie Bradshaw in *Sex and the City* who appears to be sweet, friendly, and kind; however she is an unreliable friend who expects others to take care of her, is dishonest in most of her relationships, irresponsible with money placing appearance above all else, and often plays the victim.

If you're reading this and a person or multiple people have come to mind, write their names down and take notes as you read through this book. Chances are, if their names have come to you, they are toxic in some way or are at least worth a closer look. Naz Beheshti, CEO, wellness coach, and author of *Pause. Breathe. Choose.,* shares that, according to surveys conducted by the American Psychological Association, 75% of Americans claim that their boss causes them the most stress, creating a toxic work environment. In addition, 84% of women and 75% of men claim to have had at least one toxic friendship in their lives (Beheshti, 2020). With these high percentages combined with the changes that have overcome the world due to conflict amongst people, wars between countries, and the Covid-19 pandemic, it is important to protect your heart, mind, and soul from people who drain you.

**Grab Your Detector**

Oftentimes, people behave in relationships much like they do with addictions. When a person is addicted to a drug, the drug holds power over them; it determines when they eat, sleep, work, socialize, and isolate as it is the provider of dopamine. Once a person feels the euphoric sensation from consuming drugs, smelling cookies baking in the oven, having sex, or going shopping, they'll crave it—mind and body. Especially in people with a low self-worth, the addict will do things out of character to hold on to that good feeling, much like people do in unhealthy relationships. In these relationships, there is always an imbalance; one person giving more than receiving (Solferino & Tessitore, 2019). In order to get to the bottom of the reason for the attachment developed toward toxic people, one needs to examine life from all angles.

Chances are, if there is a toxic person in your life, you may be accepting more than you currently realize. This is not to place blame on anyone as it is preferable to believe that people do the best with the tools they are given. The information within these pages aims to provide you with the tools to break free from unhealthy cycles by noticing them, understanding where they stem from, what brings you back or holds you in place, and moving into the authentic version of you with the confidence and drive to accept nothing less than what you deserve and desire.

To understand whether a relationship is toxic or not, we must often be honest with ourselves so that we can safely remove the rose-colored glasses and see the other person's behavior for what it really is. Often we do not know what to look for or where to begin looking. Some of you reading may be fighting the urge to flip pages for the section that tells you how to avoid these relationships or how to get out of a current one, and I'm here to advise you to slow down and take inventory. Cutting people out of your life may be necessary and highly beneficial in some cases, but it is not always the answer. Below, a variety of scenarios are provided exhibiting toxic relationships within family, friendships, romantic, and work relationships. As you read the scenarios, keep a journal handy and jot down anything that comes to mind, no matter if it is a fleeting thought or something more obvious.

## *Family*

Rafi is a quiet teen who has a small and tight-knit friend group. He plays badminton and soccer, is part of the chess club at school, and gets average grades. Rafi's parents often compare him to his sibling, Nala, who is popular, gets good grades, plays basketball, is on the swim team, student council, and participates in drama club. Rafi comes home from school happy but dreads sitting at the dinner table when the family comes together to discuss the day's achievements and struggles because he knows at least one of them will make jokes at his expense.

"Okay, Nala, Rafi, you know the drill," Mom says. "Share your highlight of the day and one challenging bit."

"I—" Rafi began, but was immediately silenced by his mom.

"Let Nala go first, Rafi. She had her big swim meet today and we want to hear about it."

"But, I had my second badminton tournament and—"

"Rafi, listen to your mother. Nala goes first," Dad says.

Rafi is used to this, being shut down resulting in feelings of resentment toward his sister and frustration toward his parents. Nala goes on to talk about her swim meet, where she won first place and, of course, doesn't have a challenging bit to add. Sitting up straight, accepting the praise from her parents and Rafi who congratulates her on the win. When Rafi speaks up, the family slouches, the dad rolls his eyes and says, "Alright, Rafi. How was your badminton tournament?"

"Yeah, did you come in last again?" Nala snickers.

"I actually played so much better this time," Rafi explains, "I came in fourth place and my coach said—"

"Fourth isn't really something to be excited about. Why can't you train harder like your sister and come in first place?" Mom asks, and the family laughs at Rafi's expense.

Rafi tries to brush off their laughter and continues with his challenging bit of the day. "A kid made fun of me at recess today and I—"

"What's new, Rafi?" Nala asks. "Kids are always making fun of you during recess."

"I hope you stood up for yourself this time instead of whining to the teacher," Dad says.

Rafi lowers his head and stops talking. The family goes on with their conversations and occasionally asks for Rafi's input. When Rafi refuses to participate, they brush him off as being reclusive and grumpy; two things he was not prior to interacting with the family.

In this scenario, Rafi experiences toxicity from all family members. Notice how everyone takes a turn diminishing Rafi's achievements and challenges through criticism and cruel remarks. Their behavior toward him shows a lack of empathy and the parents are creating conflict between Rafi and Nala by comparing the two in negative ways. While this example shows one familial interaction, a toxic family member might display these toxic traits in more subtle ways, such as quiet comments, sharing your business with others without your consent, or continuously ignoring your boundaries (Vincenty, 2021).

## *Friendship*

Toxic friendships are all too common and might be difficult to detect at first glance or from the outside. Think about the friends you spend the most time with and ask yourself: *Do I feel drained or energized during and after spending time with them? Do they build me up and celebrate my accomplishments or do they brush over them or immediately state something they have done that may be viewed as more important?* These questions should give you a bit of an idea of how much toxicity you allow in your friend groups. Of course, no one has good days all the time, we all make mistakes and say or do things that we later regret. A person who is just having a bad day will likely reach out to apologize later, while a toxic person does not show remorse and may even dismiss you if you bring up something they did that hurt you. A person having a bad day aims to improve their behavior choices; a toxic person couldn't care less about how you feel (Lamonthe, 2022).

Notice how your friends speak about you and to you. It is natural for friends to tease each other, but a toxic friend often puts you down in front of others, makes jokes at your expense, and leaves you feeling embarrassed or miserable. For example, you start seeing a new romantic partner and your friend makes jokes at your expense in front of them, then, when you approach them about how this makes you feel, they tell you you're sensitive and everyone knew they were joking. "Lighten up." Perhaps you stayed up watching TV all night and the next day you look really tired with your hair disheveled and clothes buttoned incorrectly. A true friend will likely not comment on your appearance because it doesn't matter, they may tease you for being "addicted" to a new show, but a toxic friend will likely put you down, starting with your appearance and then making fun of your interests (Everly, 2019).

A toxic friend may rush to your side when you are struggling but downplay your happiness out of jealousy. This type of friend may even distance themselves when you are experiencing joy as they prefer to feel as if they are better than you; likely coming back to you in a time of need. Meanwhile, they'll still like and comment on your social media posts and act like nothing has changed (Everly, 2019).

A good friend is able to debate topics with you; good friends can argue without attacking one another personally. A toxic friend needs everyone to be on their side, to believe what they say, and will likely turn anything not in line with their expectations or opinions into a fight where they attack you personally. For example, if you share something with them that you've learned through a book or documentary they'll respond with "Are you sure?" "Did you read/watch the whole thing?" "How do you know the source is credible? It's probably better to ask Google."

Take a look at your friends and note if they fit into any of the above scenarios. Ask yourself, *Does this person truly care about me? Are they there for me when I need them? Do they only call when they need something? Do they make me feel guilty if I'm busy?* If you've answered yes to the last two questions, it's likely the friend in mind exhibits toxic behaviors.

## *Romantic Relationship*

A healthy romantic relationship will feel easy, comfortable, and free. In a healthy relationship, you and your partner respect each other and choose to love each other unconditionally. Many people throw that word around without really understanding its meaning. To love unconditionally doesn't mean you never disagree or spend time apart and that you're in a honeymoon phase all the time, it means to accept a person as they are and as they evolve. To give each other space to be yourselves and partners without breaking each other's spirits or denying feelings. Most decisions are made together, you talk about problems or obstacles as they arise, and you enjoy spending time together engaged in activity and conversation, or happily doing your own things in each other's presence (Lamonthe, 2022).

A toxic relationship will not feel easy or like it's working. If you've been in one, you know the feeling already and might roll your eyes or even shed tears remembering how being in this position feels. In a toxic relationship, you and your partner likely argue about the smallest of things. Maybe you left your dishes on the counter instead of in the sink, where you always put your dishes, but tonight you were distracted by a phone call. In a healthy relationship, the partner might joke about it, remind you, or just put them in the sink without mentioning it, but a toxic or resentful partner might turn this into a big argument attacking you and your ability to keep a clean environment, perhaps bringing in old arguments that have since been put to rest. Some of you may read this and think, *uh oh, am I a toxic person? I hate that my partner assumes I'll do all the cleaning and I yell about it sometimes*. This is actually still an example of a toxic partner because mature, healthy people know that they are responsible for themselves and their environment. Only a selfish, toxic person assumes home maintenance is the job of one person and not the responsibility of everyone in the living space (Lamonthe, 2022).

Nothing you do will ever be good enough for a toxic partner and they will ensure you know this by saying things under their breath or downplaying something that excites you privately or publicly as they know no boundaries. For example, maybe you left your high-paying job to be a writer and you published your first book! You are so excited to share this achievement with your partner and upon hearing it they hug you, say congratulations, but then point out that it's only an e-book and it'd be way cooler if you had a hardcopy in a bookstore that people could actually see. Logically, you know that an e-book is an awesome achievement and that millions of people buy and read e-books every single day. The hard reality is, that for some people, emotions take over logic and they begin to doubt themselves, no longer feel proud of their achievements, and feel small in comparison to their partner due to their lack of support.

Do you feel nervous around your partner? Do you watch what you say to avoid a reaction from them? Do they often forget dates or events scheduled and act like it's no big deal or blame you for not reminding them sooner? Does your partner dismiss your needs by interrupting the conversation to tell you that you are too critical or say that they never do enough for you, making you feel like you're the one who should apologize and do better? If these questions describe your partner, it is a good time to rethink your relationship and what you are gaining from it. You can still love a toxic person and know that you deserve better treatment and more respect; if they are not able to give that to you, go find someone who can (Lamonthe, 2022). Dating is anything but easy, that is, until you meet someone who truly loves who you are and isn't trying to change you or benefit from your success or downfalls. Love isn't supposed to hurt.

## *Work Relationship*

According to the MIT Sloan Management Review a study conducted between April and September 2022 revealed that a toxic work culture is 10.4 times more likely to result in people resigning than any other factor, ranking high above even that of job security and financial compensation. The same team states that a toxic work environment can be defined by a number of factors that include but are not limited to "a failure to promote diversity, equity, and inclusion; workers feel disrespected; and unethical behavior" (Sull et al., 2022). Jennifer Moss, an Ontario-based international public speaker, author, and member of the UN Global Happiness Committee, wrote that there are signs you can look for to determine whether or not your workplace is toxic (Moss, 2021):

- speaking up and not being heard
- gossip and rumors
- bullying
- favoritism

- narcissistic leadership
- unsustainable workloads

In an article written for CBC News, Moss points out that it may not be the workplace that is toxic but the people. For example, you could work at a wonderful company who supports your growth, encourages you, celebrates you, and compensates you fairly, but there is one employee who is never happy and is always critisizing the workplace. Whether it be coworkers, administration, or the company itself, the toxic employee is someone who dislikes their job and makes sure you dislike it too. The toxic employee will likely display no loyalty toward the company or coworkers, they won't conduct themselves professionally or follow ethical standards, and may only develop "friendships" or work relationships if offered favors or anticipate that their association will help them advance (Moss, 2021).

Workplaces are not going to be perfect pictures of joy, inclusion, and happiness at all times and everyone, no matter their job or position, needs to vent their frustrations at some point, but a toxic worker or boss will complain more often than others, is never happy, and often brings stress to work which only makes matters worse; they add to the problem instead of offering solutions (Moss, 2021). Unless you feel safe, supported, and heard more often than not, it is likely that you are working in a toxic environment. In the past, employers have resulted to a "customer's always right" approach in running their company or business; however, this is not always the case and employees deserve the support of their superiors (Perna, 2022).

For example, perhaps you are an experienced, well-educated teacher who has a student going through a tough time and their behavior is detracking from the learning of others and you decide, after exhausting all methods available in your tool box, to approach your boss for guidance. A healthy, supportive boss will talk through the situation with you, offer suggestions for helping the student succeed, and assure you that they will support you through communication with the child's family or caregivers. A toxic boss may brush off the conversation as unnecessary and tell you to focus on the rest of the class instead of that student, they may suggest removing the student from the classroom against your knowledge that this act will only be more damaging to the student, and does not support you during meetings about the child's behavior.

Maybe you work at a fast-food restaurant and you're the youngest, newest employee there. Supportive coworkers and bosses will take the time to train you, offer a helping hand without hesitation when needed, and will make you feel welcomed and valued as a member of the team. A toxic coworker or boss won't help you even if you obviously need help, they will be negative about the company, will ignore complaints pointing out the high demands of their job compared to yours. They may criticize your performance and even let you make mistakes on purpose to make themselves look better.

Now more than ever, people are choosing to leave environments that are toxic for them or fighting for a healthy workplace by exposing its toxicity and suggesting how to move forward. It is essential for employers to strive for healthy working environments that employees are proud to contribute to because if employees are not satisfied, due to the amount of jobs available online these days, there is no longer a dire need for anyone to remain in a workplace that makes them unhappy and they will search for something better. According to MIT Sloan Management Review, the factors needed to keep employees on staff include lateral career opportunities, options to work remotely where possible, company-sponsored social events, and a predictable schedule (Sull et al., 2022).

# Chapter 2: Rope Burn

**Break Free**

Imagine you're playing tug-of-war, the other side is winning, you're gripping the rope so hard that your knuckles lose their color, you're getting splinters from the rope, and just when you go to catch a breath, the other side pulls you to the ground and you're left with wounds to nurse while the opposing side celebrates their victory. Staying in a toxic relationship can have a similar impact; the toxic person demands more from you than you can bare, criticizes your choices and opinions, diminishes your self-worth all while you strive to make them happy, yet no matter what you say or do, that "rope burn" never really has a chance to go away. Once one fight is lost, another begins, and the cycle continues.

Breaking free from a toxic relationship is a lot easier said than done; it is proven that once you take pride in yourself and value who you are at your core, it is easier to set boundaries that protect you from the negativity that comes from continued toxic relationships. It may be simple to avoid toxicity once you begin to notice red flags, especially if you've escaped a toxic relationship in the past, but how do you let go of a toxic relationship with someone you love and care for, someone you've known for years, someone you've already developed a relationship with? It won't be easy, but it will be worth it. The biggest question to ask yourself is, "Do I feel more pleasure or pain when I am with this person?"

Are you in relationships with friends, family, or romantic partners where you are hoping they reach the potential you see in them, that they'll go back to who they used to be, or are you seeing them as they are? A huge reason why people stay in or keep toxic relationships is out of hope that this person will become who they need them to be, and even if the person doesn't change, they've gotten so used to having them in their lives that the thought of cutting them out hasn't occurred. Below you will find three types of toxic relationships and why they hold such a tight grip on our hearts.

### *Romantic Partner*

There are a number of reasons why people stay in a romantic relationship even when it is unhealthy. For example, some people may not know what love should feel like or what makes a healthy relationship. Family dynamics and the types of relationships you had and were exposed to throughout childhood impact the relationships you develop in your life outside of the family unit. Perhaps your caregivers were often arguing or had an imbalance of responsibility between them; if this is the case, it is likely that you subconsciously associate arguing and inconsistency, possibly even abuse, with a loving relationship. In turn, you find it difficult, if not impossible, to leave. Maybe one of your caregivers always strived for affection from the other, often being turned down; this could instill an idea that you should stay in a relationship because you believe you should beg for love and affection, that it is not given freely, or you believe this is how love is supposed to be. Examining your parents' or caregivers' romantic relationships can provide insight into your own patterns of dating and ideas about love (Martin, 2019; Zarrabi, 2022).

Many who were not privy to witnessing or being part of healthy relationships in their childhood are likely to develop an anxious attachment style whereby they are so worried that the person will abandon them that they hold on tight, tend to take small things very personally, and need frequent confirmation of the bond shared. Along with anxious attachment comes a fear of being alone and leads one to believe that it is better to have someone than no one. This person will stay in a relationship no matter what and it is likely that, unless they seek guidance from outside the relationship, they will choose to remain unhappy instead of pursuing a new life, free from the toxic partner (Steber, 2019; Zarrabi, 2022).

It is highly likely that the person reaching or begging for affection from their partner has a low sense of self-worth, possibly due to treatment from their partner or they went into the relationship with an already low sense of worth that was exacerbated by their toxic partner. Your mind is a powerful source that will act on whatever you feed it and will perceive the world in the tone in which you speak to yourself or allow others to speak to you. If your self-talk is always self-deprecating, it is likely that you will accept and even believe this talk from someone else. The more productive and positive your inner dialogue, the more often you will feel happiness, the more you will attract this kind of talk from others, and the less likely it is that you will accept self-deprecating talk as fact and approach it instead with confidence and question (Steber, 2019).

Changing your thought patterns is not an easy endeavor; it takes dedication, work, and strength that can be rebuilt even after years of being beaten down. The low self-worth that often accompanies a toxic relationship can make leaving feel pointless because you have convinced yourself that no one will love you anyway. Low self-worth can also lead one to believe they are the reason the relationship isn't working and blame themselves to a point that the toxic person behaves however they like, disregarding their partner's feelings or trying to reassure them that their thoughts are incorrect because the toxic person is selfish and are in the relationship because they get something without giving (at the same frequency) in return. Therapist and licensed counselor, Matt Smith, suggests pinpointing your core beliefs and identifying their self-limiting properties in order to move forward and develop self-confidence. Once you recognize what holds you back, you are able to create a new path forward, develop your idea of what a loving healthy relationship is, and finally begin your pursuit of happiness learning that it comes from within and can either be amplified by healthy relationships or destroyed through toxic attachments (Steber, 2019).

Another reason someone may stay in a toxic romantic relationship could be that the thought of starting over, having to date, and/or being a parent alone can feel like a task so daunting that you choose toxic familiarity over fear. The attachment you feel toward someone often makes leaving or bringing up hardships very difficult and can feel like an impossible and threatening task. If you have spent many years investing in a relationship with someone incompatible, you have likely given up parts of yourself to make it work. Spending time getting to know yourself outside of the relationship and learning to enjoy time in solitude can help rebuild your self-confidence (Steber, 2019).

In cases where a child is involved, there is a whole new set of fears that come along with ending the relationship with the other parent. These fears can include, but are not limited to, loss of full custody or fear of not being there for your child, the financial responsibilities and obligations that come from being single, emotional and/or physical abuse and the fear of retaliation, fear that your child's happiness will negatively be impacted by the separation, and even fear of being stuck and needing permission to move about the world freely with your child.

While all of those are legitimate fears, something to consider is what the child may be learning from the continued participation in an unhealthy relationship. Are they seeing a loving bond or are they learning that love is supposed to hurt? Are they benefitting from your toxic partner in any way? Sometimes, the toxic person does not treat their child in the same way they treat the other parent, in these cases, the fear of having to coparent while living apart may be too much to bare. No matter the situation, it is important to consider how you can be at your best for your kids and give them a loving parent if you are in an unhappy, toxic relationship that leaves you tired, mentally unwell, and feeling defeated. Chances are that your child is not going to receive the best from you or your partner if conflictive energy is looming in every room.

For anyone reading this and feeling trapped, scared, or frozen, please reach out to a family member, close friend, an online community, a therapist, lawyer, or anyone at all outside of your home that can provide a listening ear, an understanding mind, and a willingness and love to help you through whatever decisions you choose to make for your safety and mental health.

## *Family*

Toxic relationships within the family are difficult to navigate. It is ingrained in us to keep the family unit together, to be loyal to our family, and any deviation from the traditional view is deemed wrong, weak, lazy, or mean-spirited. Not all toxicity is apparent and, in some cases, those who seek validation outside of themselves are met with doubt and rejection (Martin, 2019). For example, maybe you have a different body type from your family members and they are hyper focused on diet culture while you are trying to learn to love and appreciate your body for what it is, as it is. You decide to bring up the fact that diet culture talk is not in line with what you believe and is harmful to you. Those within a healthy family dynamic will be apologetic and make a conscious effort to keep those conversations at bay when you are around. Within a toxic family, you may be met with denial, defensiveness, and ultimately a disregard for your feelings as the person or people scramble to explain away their hurtful behavior.

If the home in which you were raised was toxic, it is likely that you have developed toxic behaviors yourself or that you have developed a low sense of self-worth. In this case, chances are you don't perceive or acknowledge that the behavior is toxic or harmful and may believe it is normal or something that everyone deals with. If someone outside the family points out toxic behavior to you, you might dismiss it or offer excuses for the behavior in question as it has become your norm; however, the norm doesn't have to exist forever and it doesn't have to be viewed as normal behavior (Martin, 2019). If families are meant to love each other, a healthy family should make space for everyone's individuality and meet them with support and desire to understand. If you always feel like you're walking on eggshells and being careful about what you say, do, or wear, chances are you are amongst toxic family members.

Another element that can keep someone from approaching or cutting ties with a toxic family member is the fear of unknown repercussions. Many fear who else they may lose if they decide to stop interacting with a certain family member. They may ask themselves if they'll be included in family events; if they want to be, what traditions will be lost or what opportunities will be gone if they no longer involve the toxic person in their lives? Of course, it is always easier to stick with what you know and keep on going as you always have, but ask yourself who this benefits (Martin, 2019). The amount of time you dedicate to building and maintaining toxic relationships determines the state of your mental health. How far will you let it go? How much is too much? When is enough, enough? If family toxicity is your reason for picking up this book, I'd say that you've had enough and are ready to leap into the unknown by choosing your own happiness over that of pleasing people who are hurting you. Let the fear drive you forward rather than hold you back.

We often hear that love should be unconditional and that if you truly love one another you'll take the time to work through any hardships. However, this idea can lead people to put up with harmful behavior in an effort to demonstrate their unconditional love. This kind of thinking can lead one to explain away poor behavior, to silence their feelings in efforts to "keep the peace," and keep toxic family members in your circle for no other reason than biological ties. No matter the nature of the relationship, take notice of how often you succumb to behavior that leaves you feeling sad, empty, or alone. If you cannot recall a recent time when your family member displayed healthy relationship patterns, chances are they're showing you who they are and you're choosing to ignore it. While it is possible to rebuild relationships after toxic behaviors are pointed out, it is likely that the toxic person in question lacks the self-awareness to pick up on their behavior and may even blame you by calling you sensitive or unappreciative (Martin, 2019).

The biggest element that keeps us in any relationship is love. The existence of toxic behavior does not eliminate love; love can change and grow, love can accept and let go. Letting go or cutting ties is not easy, definitely does not feel loving, and might not be the right choice at this moment in your life; however, if television and movie dramas have taught us anything, it is that love is not enough. Maybe you are the caregiver to the toxic family member, maybe you feel obligated to stick around because they are, afterall, family. It can be difficult to let go of the relationship, of the hope that it will one day be good or, perhaps you can recount numerous happy memories with this person and hope that new memories will be created together. Ending the relationship or setting firm boundaries with the toxic family member probably feels unloving, but if you're here, it's likely that you don't feel love from them either. You can love someone immensely and still not be able to have a healthy relationship with them (Martin, 2019).

*Friendship*

A friendship may not start out as toxic and you may have years of happy memories together, but somehow over time you have lost that feeling of joy and ease. Where you once felt excited to spend time with them, you now find yourself dreading interactions, avoiding them at school or at work. Maybe no one notices the changes except for you because they are subtle. Though your friend's behavior is hurting and confusing you, you still keep this person in your life. Why might this be? Is it due to your history? Are you afraid of the repercussions in your friend group? Do you try to convince yourself that they're just going through a tough time and they'll come around eventually? Maybe your best friend is your sibling or cousin, maybe you've known them since elementary school and their family has been friends with yours for as long as you can remember and you worry what it'll do to everyone else's relationships. The so-called end of an era is a difficult thing to fathom and being the one to end it can be emotionally crippling.

It is easy to romanticize the bond and remember all of the good times that you've shared rather than focus on the hurtful details. The thought of not having this person in your life, despite the way they have been treating you, may seem unrealistic and unnecessary; that is, until you really step outside of the history you share and view your friend and the relationship between you as it is right now. When was the last time you felt happy with this friend? Do you feel that your friend is not reliable anymore even though you continue to be? Do they demand that you be available to them at all times, but are never there for you? Are you left feeling guilty or gloomy after parting ways? Is your friend criticizing you or questioning your intelligence by disrespecting your boundaries (Merinuk, 2022)?

Regardless of the time you've spent together, the fond memories you share, and the mutual connections, you are not living in the past or the future; you cannot change or forget what has happened between you; you cannot predict the future, but you can choose your present path. Do you feel like you are putting in a lot of effort to maintain your friendship and attempt to communicate your point of view frequently, yet your friend acts as if they couldn't care less, like nothing is wrong, or blames you for the way things are going? If this friend is not putting in the effort or listening to you when you are vulnerable with them, you could step back. This doesn't mean ignoring them, but to stop trying so hard to make it work. By making an effort on par with your friend, you may feel relieved of the pressure to fix everything or to keep the peace. Friendships and relationships of any kind ebb and flow and maybe the reality is that it just isn't working right now and that could be their fault or no one's fault as people grow and change as they age, go through different experiences, and meet new people. Stepping back might allow you space to breathe again, to notice what you like about yourself and what you need in a friend; you could foster other friendships or try something new; spend time alone to learn that you are good company too (Merinuk, 2022).

While there are many reasons people keep toxic friends, stay in toxic relationships, or resist cutting family ties, a big factor in keeping one "locked in" is that of emotional abuse. This type of abuse is not solely represented in romantic relationships but in friendships and family relationships as well and it isn't until we begin to work on ourselves that we notice or agree to label the relationship as unhealthy and emotionally abusive. Many of the combined behaviors outlined in the above sections illustrate a form of emotional abuse that can make leaving someone very tough. Signs of emotional abuse include heightened criticism and judgment, manipulation and gaslighting, possessiveness and other controlling behaviors, complete disregard for your boundaries, often dismissing your feelings in the process, and invading your privacy (Koza, 2017).

As a result, the recipient of emotional abuse often views themselves as the problem as opposed to the behavior from their friend, family, or partner; they tell themselves they are deserving of this because they have done something to provoke it. Emotional abuse can look like guilting you into participating in something because it is "your role," a tradition, or using the concept of loyalty to make you feel obligated to do what is being asked or expected of you. This type of relationship can leave you like an addict, reaching for the highs and doing anything you can to avoid the lows in an effort to keep this person in your life out of fear; fear of losing the friendship, fear of how awful it'll feel for a while, and fear of trying to make new friends (Martin, 2019).

Relationships require work and communication to strengthen and last; however, there must be equal effort, not at all times, but in general it should be apparent to you that the other person values the relationship via the time and effort they dedicate to it. While disagreements are common and natural whether at home, at work, or at school, sacrificing your personal values and sense of self is never a requirement of a healthy engagement. Your relationships should be places where you can go to rest, to reset, to be yourself without reservation; a place of love and understanding no matter the act that brought you to seek comfort. Your worth is not attached to your relationship status but your relationship should make you feel worthy, and, if it doesn't, it's time to reevaluate why you're there in the first place (Martin, 2019; Zarrabi, 2022).

Oftentimes, we define ourselves by those around us, our families, our jobs, our friendships and relationships, or social and economic status. When you base your identity on the position you hold in the lives of others it can cloud the ability to see that you are enough by yourself and that you can choose the relationships you want to nourish and those you want to move on from.

**Recipe For Disaster**

I'm sure you can imagine a range of possible outcomes from staying in toxic relationships and it is often easier to spot the signs in others before we can see them in ourselves, partners, friends, or family. The desire to work through anything for the sake of the relationship is strong and sometimes unbreakable for the one grappling for affection. Staying in relationships of this nature have severe consequences to mental, physical, and emotional health. It was reported via *The Journal of Violence Against Women* that a study conducted of females living in an urban domestic violence shelter found that two key factors played a role in leaving an abusive relationship:

1. The risk assessment.
2. The level of decision certainty, both of which differed from person to person.

Interviews with residents of the shelter and statistics available revealed that reasons for returning to the abuser included, but were not limited to, a lack of financial independence, the length of the relationship, and the number of times they'd left and returned in the past. Perception is everything; if you minimize or question your pain the more likely it is that you will return or repeat the same relationship patterns (Martin & Berenson, 2000).

Learning the long-term effects of remaining in a toxic relationship can help you decide what steps you are ready to take. Leaving completely is not always the only option if both/all parties are willing to seek therapeutic guidance to get to a place of stability and compatibility; the key words being *both/all parties* (Arene, 2021). Therapy can help you build your self-esteem and provide you with the tools to come out of the dark, but it cannot fix or guide your relationship unless all parties are involved and committed to the healing process. So, you need to ask yourself what you want to do; work on the relationship or move on?

After being in a long-term toxic relationship, your personality changes little by little as time passes until one day you see yourself through the eyes of the toxic person or people in your life; you no longer know who you are because they have broken you down over time, manipulated and destroyed your sense of self. When this happens, you no longer believe or accept compliments from others, you may begin to self-isolate due to feeling inadequate, suffer from depression or anxiety, and the toxic partner will make you feel guilty for this sad state you are in even though their behavior drove you to this point. To come out of this darkness can take years of therapy and self-work, but nothing is impossible (Arene, 2021).

Another effect of long-term toxic relationships can result in what Elaine N. Aron, scientist and author, refers to as the undervalued self. Dr. Aron studies the psychology of love and close relationships and states that through the process of being broken down by a romantic partner, friend, or family member one begins to rank themselves much lower than they would have before this relationship, and creating new links or bonds within that relationship or with others becomes increasingly difficult. She explains that everyone has a process of linking and ranking; linking refers to the emotional bond you share with another and ranking is how you compare yourself (Aron, 2010) .

In long-term dysfunctional relationships, whether they be romantic, familial, friendly, or work-related, it is likely that the person receiving abuse ranks themselves consistently lower in the relationship and in other areas of their lives. The low sense of self-worth that seeps in over time beats a person down to what can feel like nothing; a ghost of yourself. Some reading may be so deep into self-loathing that they believe that the rank they give themselves is fact rather than a matter of perception. If this is where you are, I invite you to make a list of the people you see or interact with the most in your daily life and ask yourself how much do you focus on the bond, the love between you and how much do you focus on the differences between you, putting yourself below them via appearance, occupation, relationship status, intelligence, etc.? In a mind free of self-doubt and free of toxic relationships, there would be more linking than ranking, whereas a mind full of self-loathing has more ranking than linking. The fact that you rank yourself lower than someone doesn't mean the relationship is unhealthy, it means that you have a distorted sense of self and need to undo the damage caused by past or present experiences (Arene, 2021; Aron, 2010).

Not only does the above take away from present happiness, it distorts your ability to receive love from others. No matter their intentions, your sense of self has been so hurt that you doubt the sincerity of others as a way to protect yourself from potential harm. This can happen subconsciously and it isn't until you begin to work on yourself that you will notice how you interact with the world due to the negative experiences you've had. Healing is a very slow process, but it is imperative that you stick to it because you are worthy of living a happy life. You'll know you're starting to heal when you become conscious of your thoughts and can identify where they come from. Once we notice inner dialogue, we can work on changing the narrative. In some instances, the dramatic escape is unnecessary but only you can decide this. If you are not ready or do not feel it necessary to walk away, then something you can do is to be vocal about your feelings and set boundaries where necessary. People who truly love you will respect your new sense of self and act accordingly; people who are toxic or abusive will disregard your attempts and continue to diminish your self-worth (Arene, 2021; Aron 2010).

If the above isn't enough of a blow, there are numerous other ways that toxic relationships can impact your overall physical and emotional health. Researchers from the University of Michigan found that high blood pressure was directly associated with heightened levels of stress and negativity within the relationship.

While this data does not reflect all relationships, it revealed that, in a heterosexual marriage, men's blood pressure was more impacted by their partner's stress and both parties displayed heightened blood pressure with prolonged interactions. Stress messes with your body and mind in all sorts of ways like weakening the immune system which lowers your body's response to bacteria and viruses making illness and mood disorders much more difficult to treat the longer the cause, i.e. the toxic relationship, continues (Barhum, 2020).

Being in a toxic relationship often means being in a frequent state of tension where your body and mind battle the type of reaction you will have: fight, flight, freeze, or fawn. These reactions are the mind's way of protecting us in dire situations, but if you are in a toxic and abusive relationship for an extended period of time, this state of high alert causes inflammation in the body by which you are more susceptible to illness (Barhum, 2020).

*Fight*

A healthy fight response can be asserting your boundaries by not allowing someone to take a certain tone with you or treat you with disrespect, or perhaps you're on a hike and you encounter a bear. The fight response in you will protect you from the bear by helping you trap it or escape from it. The above responses protect our mind and body from potential threats in a healthy way. An unhealthy fight response would be when that feeling of being attacked never goes away, you are always on alert and in defensive mode. This feeling can be directed inward causing intense feelings of anger toward oneself or outward whereby the person is controlling, demanding, and entitled (LifeStance Health, 2022).

## *Flight*

The flight response is when one feels the need to walk away or remove themselves from a situation entirely as a matter of protection. A healthy flight response would be walking away or disengaging from harmful conversations, physically removing yourself out of danger, leaving toxic relationships, and an ability to properly assess danger. An unhealthy flight response as a result of trauma can leave one feeling that they are in danger at all times and make it difficult for them to see things as they are rather than as a threat. Someone in a constant state of flight may suffer from anxiety, they may feel the need to stay busy at all times and become a workaholic, or they may exhibit obsessive tendencies in order to keep themselves safe from danger (LifeStance Health, 2022).

## *Freeze*

While not as common as the above responses, the freeze response can be a very effective tool in processing emotions and reacting in a conscious way. For example, when confronted with conflict, some people will freeze or pause to assess the situation before reacting to it. This can result in mindfulness and awareness, allowing the person to focus on the present moment. An unhealthy freeze response to trauma may be when someone feels physically incapable of moving like when a person is repeatedly emotionally and physically abused, they may be as quiet as possible to avoid enraging their abuser. The unhealthy freeze response may present itself as zoning out, isolation, inability to focus or complete tasks, fear of the unknown, and difficulty making any decisions (LifeStance Health, 2022).

*Fawn*

The fawn trauma response is akin to people pleasing. People pleasing can be beneficial in many ways by instilling compassion for others, active listening skills, a sense of fairness, and the ability to compromise. On the other hand, the fawn response in association with trauma can lead to codependency, staying in dysfunctional and harmful relationships out of fear, the inability to set and uphold healthy boundaries, and a potential loss of self (LifeStance Health, 2022).

While the above responses are the body's natural way of responding to threats in order to protect you, being in that constant state can be detrimental to your health, your ability to recognize, build, and maintain healthy relationships, and ultimately your sense of self. Major depressive disorder can develop over prolonged periods of toxic interactions and can severely impact all areas of your life, oftentimes making day to day tasks feel impossible; as a result, you choose to isolate due to an imbalance in the body caused by external trauma. If you are constantly focused on the problems in your relationship, family, friendship, or workplace, it is likely that you have little time to focus on keeping a healthy lifestyle physically and emotionally. Without taking care of our minds and bodies, we reduce our lifespan and spend way too much time in a state unfulfilled (Barhum, 2020). All the love in the world isn't going to make something work that isn't meant to.

# Chapter 3: At Arm's-Length

**Within Bounds**

If you are a frequent reader of self-help and psychology genres, chances are you have heard about setting personal boundaries which requires a deep understanding of yourself. When a person has a distorted sense of self, they may not be able to stand up for themselves and will tolerate behavior and language that causes pain; i.e. they do not succeed in setting boundaries. When a person knows what they value, believe, perceive, and think they are better able to set limits to people that feel like a threat to their core being; i.e. they are able to say no without worrying how the other person will feel because they know in themselves that it is the right choice to ensure their well-being (Brooten-Brooks, 2022).

The ability to set personal boundaries reduces stress, burnout, and invites balance into your life. A simple example could be setting a boundary for yourself to go to bed earlier because you need more energy to get through the school, work, or parenting day instead of staying up late for alone time, to watch your show, or text with your friends. Maybe you are teaching your children bodily autonomy and you allow them to decide how they greet or say goodbye to someone. If they don't want to hug grammy, that doesn't mean they don't love her; there are plenty of ways to show affection that can allow the child to feel in control of their personal space like a high five, a wink or a wave, a choice of words like "I love you," "Can't wait to see you next time," or "Drive safe" (Brooten-Brooks, 2022).

A well-known example of an actor setting a personal boundary is when Jonah Hill posted on social media requesting that people stop commenting on his body and assuming things about his health, whether positive or negative, stating that it was harmful and not at all helpful (Thompson, 2021). It is likely that you also have been affected by diet culture standards in some way and perhaps you've had to assert boundaries of this nature within your friend groups, family, workplace, or relationship. When our appearance is criticized it somehow reduces our sense of worth by focusing on our bodies. If you surround yourself with people who are hyper-focused on their appearance, it is likely that you will be highly critical of yourself and that doesn't serve anyone. Setting a boundary in this scenario could sound like refusing to participate in diet and exercise-focused conversation, requesting that weight not be a topic of conversation around you or your children as you wish to instill body neutrality, so they learn that their worth is not tied to their appearance. This is not mean, it is not rude, it is an act of self-preservation.

Michelle Brooten-Brooks, licensed marriage and family therapist, writes that there are three types of boundaries (Brooten-Brooks, 2022):

1. Clear boundaries that are understood, flexible, and adaptable and are met with warmth and support from the family and each member feels that they can assert their boundaries without fear.
2. Rigid boundaries that are like huge impenetrable walls making it difficult for any family member to communicate their needs or even be the truest version of themselves.
3. Open boundaries are loose and unclear often resulting in codependency. Open boundaries fluctuate and are often ignored or dismissed out of the need to keep the peace.

While all play a role, clear boundary setting and open-mindedness go hand-in-hand in being yourself, respecting yourself, and allowing others to do the same.

Some boundaries are easily set and accepted by everyone such as those resulting from societal norms like property boundaries—literal lines that it is common courtesy not to cross—or boundaries on public transportation—you're not likely to sit on someone's lap if a seat is unavailable. Emotional boundaries are more difficult to set and maintain and people often forego setting boundaries out of the desire to please others. For example, if your workload is already full but a coworker asks for help, you say yes even though you don't feel like you have time, or your boss asks if you can stay late multiple times a week and you do so without complaining, but you're exhausted and running on coffee and lack of sleep. Maybe you are struggling financially but a friend group has been going out to dinner once a week for as long as you can remember, so you continue to go even though you can't afford to and know how much stress it will cause you rather than being honest and asking if they can do dinner at home instead (Faitakis, 2021).

Some worry what will happen when they set boundaries with loved ones: What if they get mad at me? What if they leave me or don't want to be my friend anymore? What if I'm just overreacting? If any of the above happen when you set a boundary, it is a clear sign that that person somehow benefitted from the lack of boundary in place and is therefore creating an unhealthy relationship and not worth hurting yourself to please. A way in which you can figure out if you need to set a boundary is to ask yourself if you actively avoid interactions with someone. If so, it is likely that this person is crossing a boundary you want to set but have yet to build up the courage to do so (Faitakis, 2021).

There are numerous types of boundaries that you can set to ensure that you are protected and respected. Below is a list of boundaries and scenarios that may be helpful in building your understanding.

### *Physical Boundaries*

Much like the above example of children being allowed to turn down a hug request, these boundaries relate to your body and personal space. Setting a physical boundary might sound like admitting when you're "touched out," like if you are a new parent and are not in the mood for intimacy, and requesting some alone time. Or if you are in an empty theater and someone sits directly beside you, you could request that they put at least one seat between you because you need personal space (Brooten-Brooks, 2022; Faitakis, 2021).

### *Sexual Boundaries*

These differ from physical boundaries in the sense that they are focused on your intimate personal space. Setting a sexual boundary would include what you do and do not like to do when it comes to sexual activity, timing, and partners. Someone attempting to cross your sexual boundaries would be someone who ignores your request to stop, offers unwanted attention, touch, or sexual activity (Brooten-Brooks, 2022).

### *Intellectual Boundaries*

Intellectual boundaries protect your beliefs, thoughts, and opinions. While you respect that others have differing or opposing ideas, you do not diminish their input. When an intellectual boundary is crossed it looks like someone dismissing your ideas, invalidating your points, or belittling you (Brooten-Brooks, 2022).

*Emotional Boundaries*

These boundaries focus on personal details and feelings. You get to decide what you share about yourself and what you keep private. Someone ignoring these boundaries may openly share personal information about you without consent, or they may ignore or dismiss your feelings (Brooten-Brooks, 2022). Perhaps you have recently decided to stop drinking and want to set a boundary with your party-loving friends. A healthy physical and emotional boundary to set may be a request that they not drink or discuss alcohol around you and that they refrain from inviting you to events that center on drinking. Toxic people are going to disregard this request and do as they've always done, possibly telling you to "get over it" or to "be stronger" or "your choice shouldn't affect how I choose to act." Sticking to your boundaries protects you from pain and acting in ways that are more harmful than helpful (Faitakis, 2021).

*Material/Financial Boundaries*

These boundaries are ones that are set when you feel that you are over-consuming, hoarding, overspending, or living beyond your means. A material boundary could be something like choosing not to lend electronics to others because you value them and cannot afford to replace them; or maybe your friend wants to borrow your necklace for an upcoming date, but it belonged to your grandmother and you are uncomfortable lending it. Crossing these boundaries would look like someone forcing or guilting you into lending something precious to you. Financial boundaries are similar in that you choose not to lend large amounts of money to friends or family to ensure the relationship not be tarnished, or turn down consistent invites to events or dinners that are above your desired budget (Brooten-Brooks, 2022).

***Time Boundaries***

Yes, you may have a job, go to school, take care of a family and you probably have things that need to get done on a daily basis, but you can still value and protect your time by asserting clear boundaries. For example, working within the hours for which you are paid. There are plenty of people who overwork themselves when in reality, they are in no way obligated to, but choose to do so due to societal or personal pressure. Maybe your partner wants to spend all of their time with you but for you, it's too much and you begin to resent your partner. Setting a clear boundary expressing that you rejuvenate with alone time and time spent with friends or doing an activity can help your partner feel heard while also maintaining the boundary that helps you feel respected (Brooten-Brooks, 2022; Faitakis, 2021).

Toxic people do not have your best interest at heart and the only person you can truly count on to protect your heart is you. Learning about boundaries has hopefully opened the door to standing up for yourself, knowing that your feelings and beliefs are valid and worth respecting.

## Know Your Limits

Now that you are aware of different types of boundaries and scenarios in which they may be necessary, we will explore the topic on a more step-by-step basis with focus on the four major relationships: friend, family, romantic partner, and work. Setting boundaries will look differently for everyone and in each of these relationships; the boundaries set will vary depending on the nature of the relationship and the situation itself.

### *Setting Boundaries with Friends*

Having friends who are negative and choose to engage in or start drama are not always the types of friends you want, but because of fond memories or histories you stay in each other's lives. If you are to a point where you are not interested in listening to their constant negativity or if you no longer want to hear about the drama in their life but are also not inclined to cut them out, it could be beneficial to set some boundaries. Boundaries allow this friend to remain in your life without over-taking it, and while it may be difficult to navigate for both of you at first, it will inevitably strengthen your relationship because, ideally, you will be respecting each other's wishes (Beuley Hunt, 2017).

The first step is learning that "no" is a complete sentence and you are not obligated to explain. This may be a bit harsh for you, and if so, you could follow it up with an honest explanation, just be prepared for the friend to either feel upset or worried about the friendship. For example, maybe you want to spend less time with this friend to stay away from the drama and rather than answering their every text or call, you start to answer or respond when you feel you have the mental capacity to do so. Maybe they invite you out to a party or for a walk and you don't feel like going. Rather than ignoring them or lying about being busy with other things, set the boundary that you want to have some time to yourself. This doesn't have to end your friendship, but keeps the distance needed to protect yourself from negativity (Beuley Hunt, 2017).

If you make it clear that you are uninterested in being a part of gossip, stick to your word and don't join in when this friend inevitably starts talking about other people's business. In this case, find something that you do share and focus your friendship and interactions on that. Maybe your friend is an astronomy buff and is a blast to go on nightly walks with, but they drain your energy if you go to dinner together as they whine about how difficult their life is. Your friendship does not need to dissolve, but it does need refocusing. This is not to say that you deny your friend the safe space of confiding in you, but that you know what you have space and time for and what you do not. If this new outlook and dynamic to your friendship causes more pain than relief, it may be time to reevaluate the bond you share and decide whether or not it is worth continuing. Ending the friendship is not a quick decision to be made and no one said you couldn't take a break from each other to see if you miss each other's company or not; so, take a break. Go a few weeks without spending time together and notice how you feel (Beuley Hunt, 2017).

*Setting Boundaries with Family*

Family is a complicated thing in this world because on one hand, we're taught that family is who will always be there for you or that we are expected to be loyal to our family because they raised us. On the other hand, not every family or family member earns our loyalty and not every family has raised us well. For those who are emotionally or geographically close to their family and have frequent interactions, it would be normal to have some level of miscommunication, disagreement, or to find it challenging to be around everyone at all times. However, if there is a particularly challenging family member who always leaves you feeling uncomfortable or unseen, it may be time to set some boundaries to protect your well-being. Setting a boundary to ensure your mental health is intact is necessary in all relationships and is a way of choosing how you allow people to treat you (Taylor Counseling Group, 2022).

Putting your personal needs first is not selfish, it is vital for your emotional well-being and happiness. So, if there is a person in your family who struggles in their own lives but always has advice for you to improve yours, someone who always makes comments about your appearance, or who demands that you are always available, approach them in a kind manner and firmly state what you will and will not tolerate. For example, maybe your family drops by without notice and disrupts your routine. A healthy boundary to set could be telling them that and adding that you can no longer accept company without prior notice. This doesn't have to mean planning weeks in advance to see each other, but a simple text or call to see if you're available or not. The boundaries in place are to help keep positive relationships in your life, not to exclude or push people away (Kane, 2022).

In order for any boundary to stick, it's important to demonstrate that it is not a flexible or negotiable request, it is a necessary act to maintain a healthy relationship. So, if your boundary is people not stopping by unannounced, don't answer the door when they do, or answer the door but do not let them in and explain your boundary again before closing the door. If your boundary is for someone to stop commenting on your appearance, stop them during the conversation if they begin to do so or walk away if they cannot respect your boundary. If your boundary is for people to not demand hugs from your children yet they continue to do so, you are well within your right to stop going to family functions with people who force physical interactions. If your boundaries have consequences that you follow through with, family will learn what you will and will not tolerate. If you do not follow through with the consequences, your boundary becomes more of a request that people can choose not to respond to (Kane, 2022).

Many people struggle to communicate clearly with loved ones out of fear of hurting feelings or being perceived as rude or unloving. Below is a template you can use for formulating your boundary.

"It makes me feel (emotion) when you (action). From now on, (boundary). If you can't respect that boundary, then (consequence)" (Kane, 2022).

Perhaps the hard part is over once you've stated your boundary, but now you must leave it up to the person or people in which you've communicated with, as it is their choice whether or not to respect your boundary. If they don't, are you prepared to walk away? It is important to be at peace with the choices you've made and to put your emotional well-being and mental health first. Just as it is important that the toxic person respect your boundary, it is equally as important for you to recognize their efforts. If your boundary requests that someone change a behavior they've engaged in for years, it will take time for them to change. Acknowledge their efforts, have realistic expectations, and avoid gossiping about them with others (Taylor Counseling Group, 2022).

This is not an easy task and likely will bring up a myriad of emotions but you can stand tall with your head up knowing that you have the strength to stand up for yourself; knowing you value yourself is a liberating feeling that will invite peace into your life.

### *Setting Boundaries within your Romantic Relationship*

Many people were not taught how to set boundaries at all, let alone in a romantic relationship. It is all too common that people remain in unhealthy relationships due to familial pressure, society's disapproval of divorce, worry that maybe something will change and you should stick it out, or perhaps you struggle with self-confidence. No matter the reason, setting boundaries in a romantic relationship may not be easy, but like other areas of your life, you choose how you are treated.

If you don't have examples of healthy relationships to base your beliefs on, focus on how you feel, how you wish love felt, and what you truly receive from the other person. It is important to get in touch with your feelings and begin to notice what influences them in positive and negative ways. Noticing is the first step to growth; you can't change something if you don't know what needs changing. In any relationship, it is important to be kind and considerate but not to a point where you are compromising your well-being (Eatough, 2021).

If you've been in your relationship for a long time and are just now realizing some toxic or unhealthy traits and are not sure how to approach the topic, it might be a good idea to start with something small. No one responds well to being bombarded by all of the things they are doing wrong, so take it one step at a time and focus on little changes that can help you feel safe, secure, and loved. For example, maybe you feel pressured to be intimate a certain number of times a week or perhaps you notice that when you are not intimate frequently your partner's mood changes and they are rude or dismissive. In this case, you would want to clearly communicate how you are feeling, why you are not feeling intimate, and the stress associated with the pressure makes it that much more difficult. Ideally, the person hearing this would feel upset that they are making you feel pressured to be intimate with them and want to know how they can make you feel at ease and loved. This is when you can communicate how you receive love and stress the importance of consent. Being in a relationship does not entitle anyone to your body; setting this boundary could help you feel more empowered (Eatough, 2021).

When setting boundaries with loved ones, you may be met with comments like, "Is there anything I'm doing right?" or, "All you do is complain." If this happens, it could be a cue that this person does not in fact care about your comfort but worries more about themselves, or it could be a cue for you to refocus on the boundaries you've set to maintain your happiness. Come at it from another angle by explaining what you do like and what you are okay with, while remaining firm on what is not acceptable for you. A boundary for you may not reflect the boundary of the other person as emotional and moral judgements vary. That's okay and to be expected because we all should have bodily autonomy and the power to express what we will and will not allow in our lives. Give your partner a chance to communicate their boundaries as well and respect them. If you diminish their boundaries, it is not likely that they will adhere to yours. Compassion, kindness, and self-assurance go a long way when deciding the dos and don'ts of your relationship (Eatough, 2021).

One important thing to remember and recognize is that relationships, like the people in them, evolve and change over time. What was once okay when you were younger may not be okay now and it is unrealistic to expect that your partner would just pick up on this. Leave space for exploring your limits and be vocal when lines are crossed. Some boundaries may be more flexible than others and the only way to learn the level of flexibility is to take notice of how you feel when the boundary is crossed. The level of intense emotions you feel determines how rigid the boundary should be. If your boundaries are constantly dismissed or if you disregard boundaries set by others, chances are you or your partner will become very defensive and rather than having open honest communication, resentment builds making it difficult to move forward in the relationship (Eatough, 2021).

## *Setting Boundaries at Work*

Setting boundaries within your workplace can improve your productivity, morale, and happiness while on the job. In times like these where the cost of living rises each day, putting your head down and powering through as much work as you can just to make a living is something many resort to; however, depending on your job, this may not actually be benefiting you financially. This behavior also increases burnout rates and if you work yourself into illness, chances are you will need to take time off to recuperate, defeating the purpose of overworking in the first place. So, take this as your sign to slow down, review your contracted expectations, examine how often you go above and beyond without financial compensation, and notice the impact your workload has on your relationships within and outside of the workplace (Indeed Editorial Team, 2021).

Signs of burnout may include feelings of exhaustion, lack of motivation, and loss of purpose, and these days, it may impact a lot more people than we realize due to high expectations for work performance. "The grind" is glorified in many societies and many people do not feel success unless they are busy all of the time. How often have you lied to someone about being too busy to meet up for lunch when really you were still in your pajamas and just wanted to stay home and watch tv? What about telling people you work through lunch even though you spend most of it scrolling mindlessly on your phone? Now ask yourself why you lie about taking breaks. It's likely due to the glorification of being a hard-worker and you feel that in order for people to perceive you as successful and deserving you must never take a break. Perhaps you've thought of this before or maybe it's occurring to you now for the first time, but there is nothing wrong with taking a break. I'll say it louder, THERE IS NOTHING WRONG WITH TAKING A BREAK!

If your friend or your child told you that they work seven days a week, often work through their lunch breaks, and take work home, you would likely act shocked and advise them to take a break. Speak to yourself as if you were speaking to your friend. Some of you may roll your eyes at this while others will nod their heads in agreement. If you're of the eye-rolling crew, I invite you to try setting and maintaining a time boundary with your work. For example, if you work through lunch every day, don't do that tomorrow; tomorrow, you will take your lunch break, the entire thing, and you will eat good food, perhaps walk outside, talk to a friend or coworker, do anything besides work.

Make it a goal to take at least one real break every single day and notice how your mood and productivity improve. If you're feeling exhausted and overworked, take the above boundary a step further by reviewing your contracted working hours; if the contract says your hours are 9-5, follow those hours. Sure, arrive a few minutes early to get coffee and settle in, maybe stay a few extra minutes for goodbyes or tidying up, but do not work outside of the set paid hours. When your boss or coworker inevitably asks you to stay late, come in early, or work through a lunch break, state your boundary and politely decline, knowing you are well within your rights. This doesn't mean that you'll turn into a person who never helps anyone because the hours don't allow for it, it just means that though you are willing to help others, you also prioritize your well-being by setting time boundaries (Eatough, 2021; Career Contessa, n.d.).

Another scenario in which boundaries may be helpful would be if you find your boss or coworkers reprimanding or criticizing your work in front of others; no matter the tone, if this is upsetting to you, it is important to voice that. You could request a meeting with whomever is crossing the line and communicate how you prefer to receive feedback; professionally and in private. Perhaps you find that another coworker is consistently in a bad mood or complaining and gossiping about the workplace and their negativity impacts the quality of your day. Just as this person's negative energy can influence your day, a positive energy can influence theirs. It is normal for people to need to vent or get something off their chest and boundary setting doesn't mean that you'll never lend an ear to a struggling coworker, but it does mean that you will not be a sponge for negativity. Inform this person that their constant negativity makes it difficult to do the job and you will no longer participate in drawn out complaining sessions or gossip. You can confirm this boundary by reminding them when they start complaining that you'd rather talk about something else, or walk away if they cannot help themselves. Set a personal emotional boundary for yourself by not participating in workplace gossip and keeping a positive attitude when possible to help improve your mental health and the workplace environment (Selva, 2018).

# Chapter 4: Time to Detox

**Snip Snip**

The first part of this book is all about boundaries; what they are and how to set and maintain them, but what if a person constantly disrespects your boundaries? If this is happening to you, it might be a sign that distancing yourself from this person and cutting them out of your life is the next move to make. This is harsh but it is also necessary to limit the amount of toxicity you allow into your life for the betterment of yourself and those in your circle. It is important to keep in mind that toxicity is unavoidable and that it is our reaction to it that we can control. For example, maybe you'll have to put up with being in the same space as the cousin who you wanted to cut ties from for the sake of family events, or perhaps you're going through a divorce and while you'd like to cut the other person out completely, you have a child together so it is likely that cutting them off is not possible. In these scenarios, you can remain kind without inviting the person into your life again (Harbinger, 2022).

Another important distinction to make is between toxicity and poor decision-making. Not everyone who makes bad choices or hurts your feelings is toxic, so before you start cutting people out or pushing them away, take the time to reflect on toxic traits and compare them with the frequency in which they occur and the feelings you are left with. If your partner cheats on you, it doesn't necessarily mean they are toxic, but they are definitely inconsiderate and do not deserve to be in your life. Whereas, if a sibling uses you as the punchline to their jokes, they may deserve some chances to rectify themselves by respecting a boundary you set to not poke fun at you. However, if this sibling repeatedly ignores your boundary, you may start distancing yourself from them to get your point across. Stop going to family events if they are to be present, don't attend the birthday celebration for someone who disregards your emotions; whatever you have to do to confirm your boundary is not flexible (Harbinger, 2022).

With regards to relationships, it is important to acknowledge toxic behavior and trauma experienced as well as personality differences. Sometimes, these differences can coexist and sometimes they can't. For example, if you are a person who needs to feel needed and your child or parent is a person who doesn't like to feel needed this can cause tension and conflict as one would present as overbearing and the other as distant. If discussed, it is something you could overcome with time and compassion provided both parties made an effort to respect each other's needs. If time passes and you feel like you are making changes or adaptations while the parent or child goes on behaving in the same way, this is a disregard for your feelings. So, while the person may not be toxic, they may have a personality difference that clashes with yours that puts a strain on your relationship (Harbinger, 2022). In order to know whether or not it is time to cut someone out of your life, and I'm sure if you're reading this you have at least one person in mind, the first step is to stop excusing their behavior and admit to yourself that they are an unhealthy burden (Lamoreux, 2021).

Journaling can be a helpful tool to organize your thoughts and make connections between emotions and actions. You could begin by writing about how you feel in this moment, right after something happens that heightens your emotions, or making a list of ways the person or people add to your joy, and ways they take away from it. Chances are, writing will heighten your emotions and it might be difficult to put pen to paper at first. Free writing can be an effective emotional release as well. Try setting a timer for five minutes or more and tell yourself that you are going to write whatever goes through your mind without worrying about spelling or penmanship, even if you end up beginning with, "This is dumb," or, "I have nothing to write," the process of pushing through your mental blocks can reveal feelings and answers you couldn't reach before, shedding light on the choice you knew you had to make all along (Lamoreux, 2021).

Cutting ties with someone you love is not something to do out of reactive anger but out of thoughtful consideration for your own well-being. For example, if you are living with someone who frequently lies to you, cannot admit when they are wrong, gaslights and manipulates you, yells at you, belittles you, makes unreasonable demands, etc., it is imperative that you end this relationship to protect your emotional and physical well-being. Perhaps this is not something you can do immediately as you share a home and/or finances. In this case, you can still take steps toward your exit by actively searching for a living space within your budget. If this is a matter of physical safety, talk to someone you trust and contact local helplines or authorities. Unfortunately, the number of people who need to escape an abusive situation is high, but that means that there is always somewhere to go and someone to help. Reach out, don't wait until it's too late (Martin, 2019a).

Do you have a boss who belittles, manipulates, and ignores their employees? Do you feel singled out by your boss or part of a toxic work environment? Does your boss ignore working hours, expecting you to work through breaks or come in on the weekends without extra pay? Are you afraid to go to your boss with questions, to offer suggestions, or ask for assistance? Do you feel that voicing your concerns is pointless because your boss dismisses them and rolls their eyes whenever you share your opinion? If you answered yes to any of the above questions, I'd say it's time to start seeking employment elsewhere. Many people in this situation may try to find reasons to stick around because it is familiar, it is difficult to find a new job, you may tell yourself it's okay to have a terrible boss because you know what to expect, maybe you've been with the company for years and can't fathom leaving. You have to ask yourself if the familiarity, pay, and predictability are worth sacrificing your happiness and health (Moss, 2021).

If you notice that a family member, friend, coworker, or romantic partner consistently leaves you feeling emotionally, physically, and mentally drained it is time to take action. If this is a new behavior, by all means, have a conversation and try to work through it, but if it has been a while of feeling this way, chances are it is time to let go because no one deserves abuse of any kind. Believe your instincts. The human mind is wired for protection and if you are fighting with the idea of cutting someone out or leaving them behind, chances are it is the harsh reality you should accept for your own benefit (Pace, 2022). Knowing when to cut ties is heartbreaking and difficult and you will likely second guess yourself. It is recommended that you seek the advice or counseling of a neutral party like a therapist, support group, or a trusted friend (Radin, 2020).

**No Signal**

You've journaled, talked to trusted family, friends, or a therapist and have decided that cutting ties is the only way to move forward from the unhealthy relationship, but now what? How do you go about cutting someone out completely when they've been a part of your life for however long? You may even still have love for this person and be disappointed that it has come to this because you had hoped boundary setting would improve your interactions, but time has shown that this person has no regard for your feelings and it is time to make mental health your priority by letting them go.

No, ghosting is not the answer. In case you're new to the game, ghosting means to cut ties all of the sudden with zero explanation, zero contact, as if you've fallen off the face of the earth and no longer exist. It is a cruel way to end a relationship even if that person has been cruel to you. Ghosting can cause the other person to panic and worry about you as if something drastic has happened and you're lying hurt somewhere; they may also think that the door to communication isn't completely closed. While it may feel like an easier option for those who want to avoid conflict and difficult conversations, it is a method that causes a different kind of pain and if you want your decision to stick, it's best to be open, honest, and very clear about your intentions so that you do not leave the person thinking this is temporary (Radin, 2020).

When it comes to a toxic family member whom you have attempted to reason with by setting boundaries with clear expectations and consequences yet they still behave in the same toxic manner, begin to remove yourself from the situation. Voice to them that you have tried to make the relationship work but that their disregard for your boundaries has made it impossible to continue the relationship. This person will likely engage by asking for another chance, apologizing, telling you to lighten up, or attacking your personality and poor decisions by stating all of the ways you will miss them being in your life. Do not get roped into this argument. State your decision and act accordingly.

You can choose to not attend family events with this person present, do not respond to their texts or return their calls, and mute, delete and/or block them from social media to avoid further damage to your mental health. Another difficult part of the process will be letting other family members know about your decision. Avoid gossiping about the person you've distanced from, but tell a few key family members of your decision so they are aware and understand if you choose not to attend an event. Without putting them in the uncomfortable position of choosing sides, request that they refrain from discussing you, your personal life, or this situation in detail with the other party (Radin, 2020).

Unfortunately, cutting someone off does not end your grief immediately and sometimes things can feel worse before they feel better. It is important to seek support when this happens, as what you have decided is not a small thing that will eventually be forgotten, it is a long commitment to protecting your emotional and physical health. In the case of family, i.e. a spouse with whom you've divorced or separated from, a sibling, a parent, whomever, sometimes it might not be possible for you to avoid them at all times. In this case, it would be a good plan to have a neutral party aid in the communication between you. This would mean that if you have to share custody of children, you have a third party, a trusted friend, family member, or law-figure who brings them to and from each parent or meet in a neutral public space. If you have severed ties with a parent who still provides childcare, it would be best to have someone else drop off or pick up. If you cannot have a third party do this, it is best to set firm boundaries in which you only speak of the children and their care to avoid continuous abuse or heartache. A more distant relative such as an aunt, uncle, or cousin may be present during holidays or family gatherings and it is up to you to decide if you can tolerate being in their presence in order to continue your family traditions, or if you decide you cannot, make sure your family is aware that you will not be attending due to feeling uncomfortable or unwelcome with this person and that you will be glad to see the family another time. None of this is going to be easy or feel good, but in the long run, your mental, emotional, and physical health will improve because of your ability to stand up for yourself and protect your boundaries (Radin, 2020).

If you have come to the conclusion that you and a friend are no longer compatible, the relationship causes more harm than comfort, and are ready to end the bond you share, keep in mind that this should be done when you are both in a calm state, not in a shouting match. If you cut off a friendship in the middle of an argument, the person might assume it was just something you said in the heat of the moment but didn't really mean it. They might think they have an opportunity to apologize or that you'll eventually get over it and go on as you have in the past. It is important that you are clear about your decision, the reasons for it, and that you follow through once you have made the choice to end the friendship. Without follow through, meaning without choosing not to engage with this person, they will perceive your boundaries as optional. Though you may share many fond memories together, they are not enough of a reason to continue putting yourself in situations where you end up doubting yourself (Gupta, 2021).

Ending a friendship is difficult and it may be beneficial to practice what you'd like to say beforehand so that you can stick to your decision and not get distracted by their inevitable reasoning to keep trying. Write down your reasons, perhaps use the template provided in the previous chapter by swapping 'boundary' for 'decision'. If the person is abusive, by all means, end it, block them on social media, delete their contact information, cut them out completely and don't worry about explaining. If the friendship is toxic but not abusive in any way, it is best to have difficult conversations in person rather than via text. Once you've officially told them the friendship is over and explained why, you can begin the process of ending communication and contact with this person. Request that you not be invited to things where this person will also be in attendance, remove their contact information, do not respond to texts or calls, block, mute, or delete them from your social media accounts and get on with your life, fostering healthy friendships as you move forward (Gupta, 2021).

Next up, the toxic romantic relationship. Whether you've been together for decades or only a few months, when love is involved things get extremely complicated, but one fact that never changes is the amount of respect you deserve. If you have been communicating needs with your partner, setting boundaries, and still feel as though you are a burden to them, it is time to end it and cutting ties, though difficult, will be best for you. This does not mean that you can stay friends. Staying friends with a toxic ex is not something you want to bother with because the feelings of love may not go away, they may adjust their behavior to show you they've changed to try and convince you to go back to them, and you may do so only to learn thing has changed and they are just as dysfunctional as they before. Of course, there are always exceptions to the rule; for instance, if you and your partner had an amicable breakup and have the same group of friends, staying in contact may not be so bad, but keeping them around as a potential 'backup' or if you still have feelings for them is only going to cause you more anguish. Once you are in a new relationship, continued contact with your ex may make it less likely that you will commit to the new partner, so ask yourself why you are ending the relationship and what benefits, if any, would come of staying in touch (Seidman, 2016).

Question your motives or your ex-partner's motives for staying in touch, because chances are, one of you still has hope the relationship will work out someday. Another factor to consider if your ex is the one wanting to stay in touch or who reaches out after a few months or weeks of breaking up, is whether or not their intentions are pure. If your ex was an emotionally abusive person or displayed narcissistic tendencies, it is likely that they are reaching out to you because they benefit from your connection in some way whether it be for sex, connections you have within friend groups or workplaces, perhaps they are trying to bring you back in to regain control over your mind and body. A narcissist who knows you well is dangerous; they may grab your attention by being gentle at first, such as sending a good morning text, making a phone call to see how you're doing, or asking a friend who they know will tell you they wondered about your emotional state. It may seem harmless on the outside, but they know what they are doing (Arabi, 2018; Seidman, 2016).

The most difficult thing to break is a trauma bond. Due exposure to trauma within the romantic relationship, when th is broken and contact with this person ends, your body and brain act as if they are missing something necessary to function. You may feel disoriented, lost, or lonely, you may crave the connection from this person who had such a strong influence on your emotions but rest assured, this is your body reacting to the chemical imbalance that occurs when we stop receiving those highs and lows. Over time, it will get easier, the feelings will pass, though your perception is likely altered forever due to this trauma, the feeling of wanting them back or the inability to trust will slowly dissipate as you learn more about yourself and work on building confidence. Knowing your worth, your values, and your core beliefs will make it easier to spot red flags, to avoid toxic relationships, and allow you to communicate your needs confidently in the next relationship (Arabi, 2018).

## Chapter 5: Oops. I Did It Again

**Boomerang**

I'm sure you have a friend or family member or have seen in television shows and movies people who rekindle a toxic relationship and, as an outsider, it is easy to point out their mistakes, identify the red flags, and see the relationship for what it is. However, when you are the person in it, deciding whether or not to let go or to go back, the lines become blurred and overshadowed by feelings of regret, loss, and love. We are creatures of habit and breaking routine, stopping habits, and beginning new ones is a very difficult thing to do and there are doctors, organizations, and scientists out there working on ways to help people quit the thing that is hurting them whether it be drugs, alcohol, gambling, or toxic relationships. For example, perhaps you had been married for ten years, finally gained the courage to break-up, but now you've been in the dating game for a few years with no success and the idea of going back to familiarity seems better than being alone. Be careful. It is 100% better to be alone than to go back to someone who hurt you emotionally or physically; familiarity does not equal healthy (Sells, 2019).

Some people may go back to a toxic relationship because they want to believe the person has changed and that they will give them the love and care they deserved from the beginning. While this is true in some cases, it is likely that the innate nature of the person has not changed. This is where you can refocus your thinking on personality and the toxic traits that drove you to end the relationship in the first place. As time passes or even soon after a relationship ends, it is common for people to romanticize what they lost or gave up, to only focus on the good times. It is helpful to journal or speak to a trusted friend or therapist to help you keep the facts straight and to process the difficult emotions you are experiencing. It needs to be understood and accepted that not all relationships are meant to last and that we can learn more about ourselves through each experience. For example, if you have stayed in a toxic relationship with someone who you felt you gave your all to yet they still cheated on you and then manipulated you into apologizing or accepting blame for their indiscretion, you can reassure yourself that you have learned what your heart can handle and what it cannot, and in the next relationship you will be more likely to end it if the person displays dishonest traits (Johnson, 2020).

With each loss a strength is to be gained and you may not notice this until quite a bit of time has passed or until a person you encounter exhibits similar toxic behaviors. To help yourself from repeating similar patterns, think back and journal about the personality traits this person had. Chances are that you will notice a lot more negativity than you realized prior to reexamining the relationship and the negative implications of being with a toxic partner, like low self-esteem or possible health issues caused by unnecessary stress, are enough to remind you why you cut ties in the first place. Something to watch out for when thinking about entering a new relationship or friendship is the level of jealousy displayed by this new person. Are they always needing to know where you are, what you're doing, and who you are with? Do they assume you have feelings for someone else? These are signs of immaturity and controlling tendencies and should be avoided at all costs. Disagreements are normal, going to bed angry is normal, but long-term heartache and self-doubt are not markers of a healthy bond (Johnson, 2020).

Understanding your insecurities and the things that draw your mind back to the person you've cut ties with will help you boost your self-love and compassion. Sit with your feelings instead of acting on them and try to figure out where they come from. Are you wanting to go back to an ex because you are lonely? Go out with your friends instead or invite a friend over for a night in. Are you wanting your ex back because the idea of sharing your lives together trumps being unhappy alone? Find a new hobby, ask a friend to come stay with you for a weekend, borrow the family dog to cuddle, anything to remind you that there is happiness in just being you and that the right people lift your spirits rather than break them. Notice your inner critic and shut them up by using affirmations or finding activities that bring you peace and joy, such as journaling or going to therapy. As previously mentioned, changing your inner dialogue is no easy feat and might take years to do, but if you stick with it—noticing your inner critic, pinpointing why they've surfaced, and reframing the language— you will build your self-confidence over time. For example, you've gone on a few dates with a person and have enjoyed yourself, but all of the sudden they tell you they're just not ready for a relationship right now or perhaps they ghost you altogether, your inner critic may rise and ask, "What's wrong with me? What did I do?" (Johnson, 2020).

When this happens, remind yourself that not everyone is meant to be and that you do not know what is going on in this other person's life. If they didn't say it was your fault, it likely wasn't. Rather than asking yourself what's wrong with you, roll your shoulders back, stand tall, look in the mirror, and remind yourself that you are a catch and that you don't want to be with someone who doesn't want to be with you. Just because this didn't work out, doesn't mean it won't work with the next person. Or, if the partner you returned to went back to their old ways of infidelity, instead of telling yourself they did it because you were not enough to keep them satisfied, tell yourself that you will not put up with this level of disrespect because you deserve to be loved and appreciated (Johnson, 2020).

Oftentimes, people use their relationships as a way to self-identify and when those relationships end, people can lose their sense of self in a manner so excruciating that they return to their ex to validate who they are. While there's nothing to be ashamed of, it is important to admit to yourself that this relationship is not beneficial and is likely that the return has made it even more clear as to why you left in the first place. The biggest factor to ensure you will not repeat toxic relationships is to work on your concept of self and learn how to be happy on your own so that when you do seek out a new relationship, you are no longer seeking definition or confirmation of self, but seeking joy, compassion, partnership, and love (Cope & Mattingly, 2020).

**Stronger in Numbers**

Though the value and overall importance of having good mental health is a topic more widely discussed and accepted nowadays, it doesn't mean that it is easy to seek support. Sure, there are counselors, therapists, support groups, family, friends, all of these people around you who care for you and want to help, but people often don't do anything until they're asked. What if asking is the hardest part? People who have suffered from ending a toxic relationship are often left with severe mental health issues that can range from a distorted self-image to depression and seeking help may be viewed, by them, as "just something else they can't handle". If this sounds like you, it may be helpful to know that "according to a report published by the U.S. National Institute of Mental Health, one in six American adults faces mental health problems" (Hood, 2020). This means that whether or not the person is open about their mental health struggles, it is likely that we all know someone who battles with the negative narrative their mind screams at them and if you struggle yourself, know that you are not alone.

Whether you are a teen or an adult, there are support systems available to you in person and online via family, friends, trained professions, or complete strangers. The first step to strengthening your mental health is admitting you need help in the first place. You wouldn't want your loved one to suffer alone, so don't allow yourself to do so either. If you do not have close friends, a tight relationship with your family, or the financial means to seek medical guidance, there are ways you can build a support system for yourself. Dr. Julia Hood suggests a few ways to do this by starting with determining if there is anyone in your life who always has your best interests at heart and who celebrates you. Reach out to this person and try to spend time together. Another avenue to try might be joining a local sports team, art club, or music group to pick up a new hobby or get back to one you left behind. When you're in the dark depths of depression, reaching out and being around people may be the very last thing you could imagine doing and if this is the case, you could start with building an online community instead. There are blogs, chatrooms, websites, therapists, and a whole range of online support systems that can help you get to a point where joining people in person won't feel so exhausting (Hood, 2020).

In order to improve your self-concept and learn to define yourself outside of your relationships it is useful to set personal goals to increase your motivation. Self-motivation comes from a personal desire to set and achieve goals. Everyone manages their emotions in different ways, so what might seem easy to one is difficult for the other. One might choose to make daily goals while another might choose to set long-term goals; whatever you choose, let it be something that will bring a calming sense or something you look forward to (Emamzadeh, 2022). The following are a few examples of goals you could set:

- learning a new hobby or skill
- call a friend or family member you haven't spoken to in a while
- try out a new recipe
- go for a hike, bikeride, or walk
- join a team or a club
- go on an adventure—hop on a bus or drive to somewhere local you've never been and take a walk around
- download and try a meditation app
- a work-related goal for a job you love
- join a dance class

When you're in a low state-of-mind, it's important to remain conscious of your coping mechanisms as it is easy to resort to unhealthy options like self-isolation or alcohol and marijuana. Building a healthy support system and setting achievable joy-filled goals will help you move beyond these unbearable feelings to a place of peace and self-assurance, whereas the other options merely provide short-lasting relief and cause other health issues. Ensure that the goals in which you pursue are purely joyful and do not set goals that diminish you in any way. Too many people vow to lose weight after a failed relationship as if that has anything to do with your self-worth; it does not. Setting a goal to change your body is not going to make you feel better and will likely contribute to self-deprecating talk. Set goals that you are excited about where the process is just as enjoyable as the reward (Emamzadeh, 2022).

Sometimes, we seek to restart a relationship to confirm our self-concept or we text and call many times after a breakup searching for a reason or something that will give us closure, but the truth is, even if you hear the reasons or logically know the reasons, your mind will battle with the truth in effort to avoid difficult feelings (Hood, 2020).

## Chapter 6: Raising the Bar

**Introspection**

The next step in the healing process is to acknowledge the value of objectively looking inward to examine your mind, thought processes, and feelings to help determine patterns and influences to the relationships they form. Cutting someone out or setting boundaries may have felt difficult for you and this next part may also prove to take time, but in order to move on to a place where you can engage in healthy relationships, it is vital to take a look inside yourself to gain an understanding of how your mind works. This is not about judging yourself or others, it is a conscious practice that involves seeing your thoughts and feelings for what they are; not trying to change them or blame yourself for them, just notice them and allow them to be. This can allow space for things to come up that we may not have realized before and this aids to increase our understanding of ourselves. With this heightened level of self-awareness, we are better equipped to change or alter our inner dialogue, thought patterns, and choices (Cherry, 2014; Davis, n.d.).

Introspection allows us to examine our beliefs, values, desires, intentions, and attitudes from a place of objective observance. Tchiki Davis, founder, writer, and well-being expert at the Berkeley Well-Being Institute, lists the following questions to help get you started:

- Who am I?
- Who do I want to be?
- What do I really want in life?
- How do I really feel about myself?
- What are my beliefs?
- What do I value?
- What matters most to me?
- What is the right next step for me?

These questions do not ask you to judge but are meant to help you gain a more concrete self-view. There is no right or wrong answer and some may find the questions difficult; in this case, sit with the question in your mind and notice what thoughts pop up. If it is helpful, you could journal your thoughts; chances are, the questions that cause the most resistance are the ones that will help you gain the most insight. What comes up through introspection may not always be a pleasant discovery and this is where your support systems can come in to help guide you through (Cherry, 2014; Davis, n.d.).

Something to keep in mind is that introspection can have negative side-effects; for example if you are presenting a big project idea at work or giving a speech at school and you sit with your thoughts, you may notice that you are afraid of public speaking and shame yourself for this only making it that much more difficult in the first place. In this case, introspection has not served you well, but it also points out a legitimate fear you have and this is where the work begins as you attempt to learn where this fear stems from (Davis, n.d.).

Looking back at the questions "Who am I?" and "Who do I want to be?" can provide insight into things that hold us back. For example, if you've described yourself as someone creative who is dedicated to their craft but who is anxious about sharing their work, you've learned that fear is something that holds you back from achieving larger goals like selling your artwork or approaching fairs or studios to display your work. Now that you notice this anxiety, the next time it approaches you can remind yourself of the end-goal and learn how to do it anyway despite the fear. By reflecting on these questions then adding "What do I really want in life?" you can see links to how your self-concept does or does not relate to what you want. This provides opportunities to reflect on what takes away from your desires and what adds to them, possibly giving you the drive to work through what holds you back and amplify the aspects of personality that push you forward. Asking "How do I really feel about myself?" provides insight into how you may be holding yourself back and could lead you to seek out ways to improve your self-concept through motivation, therapy, or deep conversations with trusted friends. Furthermore, reflecting on your beliefs, values, and what matters most to you can help you gain a more concrete vision of yourself and notice actions that may have deviated from this (Davis, n.d.).

Through this exercise, perhaps you learned that being successful in your job is highly important to you but when you reflect on your dedication to work, you notice that you spend more time watching television, pursuing an unrelated hobby, or taking on the massive job of running a household and family on your own. Though the things you are doing in your life that may take away from your work are not bad things, they are not helping you achieve your goal. On the other hand, maybe you recorded the most important thing in your life as love and family but, in reflection, you admit to yourself that you put more time into your job than anything else, therefore causing you to possibly lose or not create the love you wish for. There are other ways to learn more about yourself as well, such as imagining happiness by visualizing, drawing, or writing about what a happy day would be like for you (Davis, n.d.).

Introspection is about increasing your self-awareness which can provide the tools to start your journey to a more confident self, equipt with the ability to see red flags from others and within yourself. Learning from your past enables you to build a better future through increased ability to be present and conscious of the inner workings of your mind. Through this reflection, you may notice experiences that have shaped your self-concept (Davis, n.d.). For example, perhaps you had highly critical parents; if so, it would be understandable that you are also self-critical and hold higher standards for yourself or others who will inevitably not meet your expectations. This is not your fault, nor is it a sign that your parents tried to hurt you; we all do the best with what we know and when we know better, we do better. Give yourself some grace and time to change this way of thinking.

Maybe you grew up watching television shows and movies that glorified men who do as they please while the woman begs for their love. This may be an extreme generalization; however, the relationships we are exposed to throughout our lives impact the types of relationships we build, the types of people we're attracted to, and, ultimately, how we view love. This is a big 'aha' moment for many when they realize that their view of a healthy relationship is not based on actual functioning joyful bonds and can reveal that toxic behaviors that once seemed attractive are now red flags to avoid. While we cannot control or change our past, we can choose to learn from our parents' mistakes and from our own mistakes in an effort to break the cycle of toxic relationships and begin a journey of healing and growing into self-loving people.

**Brand New Me**

Now that you've set boundaries, cut toxic people out, and done a lot of self-reflection, it's time to re-develop your abilities to trust, your attitude toward relationships in general, and gain a new-found sense of self. The pain from loss might never truly dissipate, but you can learn to live with it and day by day it goes further and further into the recesses of the mind, eventually becoming a distant memory as opposed to a debilitating burden. A large part of the healing process is forgiveness; forgiving yourself and forgiving the toxic person. This is not for their benefit nor does it need to be communicated to anyone, but forgiveness can help you to move forward. This is not to diminish what you have gone through or to excuse anyone for damaging behavior, but to give yourself permission to grieve and move on by taking what you have learned and using it to become a more present and conscientious person.

As previously stated, the way one interacts with others and in the world is influenced by experiences and is susceptible to change. The way we perceive and interact within our world is a direct result of our learnings, learnings come from experiences; therefore, it could be suggested that the more reflective experiences we have, the more present and aware of our place in the world we will be. This being said, we also understand that others could experience the same thing as us but have a completely different view of what occurred and neither person would be wrong. Learning to notice compatibility, make good decisions, and build healthy relationships takes time and practice, so be patient with yourself because you are on the right track just by acknowledging that something needs to change. Not only must we ask "What happened" and "why," we must also ask "What was my part in it" and "How did it affect me?" Learning is a social practice that can be understood with the guidance of others as well as self-reflection (Fazey et al., 2005).

Oftentimes, before we can truly learn from an experience we need to process it first and this happens in stages much like the process of grief. According to psychotherapist and author, Kaytee Gillis, there are six stages of recovery after a toxic relationship and they are as follows.

**Self-doubt:** This happens in the beginning when the wound is fresh and you find yourself wondering if you are crazy, if things really happened the way you remember them. This is the part where you realize that something doesn't make sense but haven't yet figured out what that is. This is difficult in so many ways and often leaves us wondering what we did to bring out these behaviors in another person (Gillis, 2022).

**Learning and researching:** When something doesn't feel right, we can spend hours, days, or longer trying to figure it out or make sense of it. This is when you end up Googling personality traits of the person you've separated yourself from in an effort to name their mistakes and confirm for yourself that there is something wrong with them, not you. This can often bring feelings of relief as you gain a bit of clarity by being able to explain what may have happened (Gillis, 2022). It is important to be aware of how much time you spend on self-doubt and learning and researching as this behavior, if gone on too long, can be detrimental to your health. While a little will help you gain insight, an obsession can leave you feeling worse. When one spends too much time reviewing a past hurtful or traumatic experience, it can become an unconscious act to avoid being hurt in the future, but in reality, this only limits your ability to notice and feel love because you are acting and thinking from a place of fear (Leonard, 2021).

**Clarity:** The relief of knowing that what happened wasn't all your fault and some things are beyond your control. Clarity can be an empowering feeling that pushes you to seek community and help you to make choices based on love rather than fear. Before coming to this clarity, you may have noticed that you said yes to things you otherwise wouldn't have, or that you put immense pressure on yourself that was unwarranted because you feared losing something. When you learn to act with love and compassion, you can prove to yourself that you can handle things that are beyond your control by practicing acceptance for what is and looking forward to what comes next (Gillis, 2022; Leonard, 2021).

**Breaking Free:** Once you realize what or who you've been dealing with, you can break free of them by setting boundaries, cutting them out of your life, and beginning the work to become a more present and conscious version of yourself. You make a commitment to moving on, to bettering yourself, and practicing self-compassion. Meditation or mindfulness can help you through the grieving process after a big loss. Mindful eating can help bring you to the present moment by simply focusing on the task at hand rather than eating in front of the TV or while scrolling on your phone. Taking a mindful walk is a great way to break free from overwhelming thoughts. As you walk through the forest or downtown, rather than talking or worrying about what's to come, focus on the sounds around you and the feel of the ground beneath your feet (Gillis, 2022; Leonard, 2021).

**Doing the work of healing:** This is the stage you are currently in, and I can say this with confidence because you have read this far and it is a reflection of the determination you have to heal and take the journey to your "Self" by learning more about your past experiences and how they connect to current understandings of the world. This stage may be long, it may be revisited, it may be done both independently and with others. This is where you accept your faults, the faults of others, and remind yourself that, while everyone makes mistakes, you are not to blame for the way in which someone chooses to treat you. This is also the space for accepting anger. It is completely normal to feel angry after something traumatic happens and it can be helpful to channel this anger productively by expressing it through art, music, dance, or even hitting a punching bag as you imagine the rage inside of you. Anything that takes the anger from inside your body to outside will be helpful (Gillis, 2022; Leonard, 2021).

**Accepting and making meaning:** An essential part of the healing journey is to make meaning from what happened. Some people try to rush the healing journey and jump right into another relationship only to end up back in the same depressing place. Taking the time to heal by reflecting on yourself and your experiences is what helps you identify red flags in a relationship. If you do not take the time to do this, it is likely that you would repeat the same mistakes. Slow down, don't rush, feel what you feel when you feel it, and don't try to move on until you feel confident in who you are and what you have to offer (Gillis, 2022).

Practicing self-compassion is a big factor in helping you move on and change your inner dialogue. It can be helpful to keep a journal, write notes to yourself, and make time for affirmations. Affirmations are simple phrases that when repeated can become reality. For example, if you continue to look in the mirror and say, "I am ugly," it will be difficult for you to see your beauty and to accept others who compliment you. If you change this by saying, "I am beautiful" each time you pass a mirror, whether you believe it or not is not the point, by saying it you are training your mind to think positively rather than negatively and you may even start to point out things you like about yourself in the process (Leonard, 2021).

## Chapter 7: Back and Better

**You Are Worthy**

Toxic relationships can leave us feeling unworthy of love, cause us to self-isolate, and while this is a normal reaction to the ending of a relationship of any kind, make sure you don't stay there forever because there is a beautiful world out there full of kind, compassionate, trust-worthy people to be met. No matter who you are or what you look like, you are deserving of a happy and full life shared with those who have your best interests at heart. Naturally, there will always be ups and downs, mistakes and achievements, but until you heal, gain insight into your strengths and weaknesses, and decide to get back out into the world, you will continue to find those who don't match your light. You are worthy of love but not everyone is going to be able to see that; that is a reflection on them and their experiences, not you. It is so difficult not to be hurt by another's negative opinion of us, but once you heal from your past and morph into your true self, these comments will roll off your back a lot easier than they currently do.

Self-worth, self-value, self-esteem, and self-care, are terms with different yet similar meanings. Some focus on actions while others focus on internal beliefs. Having or knowing self-worth is when a person feels as though they are good and deserving of respect; relatable to self-esteem where a person has a healthy view of who they are. Self-value and self-care are more focused on actions toward yourself and others as a reflection of your values. Here, we will focus on self-worth, as this is the driving factor to how you speak to yourself and interact with the world (Ackerman, 2018).

Many people base their sense of worth on their achievements, grades, relationships, financial gains, internet followers, appearance, age, and whatever other people say about them. If you are realizing that this is what you base your self-worth on, it's time to toss those thoughts in the garbage and learn that you are more than any of those things and your worth is unchanged by success or failure. What truly reflects a person's worth is viewed in their respect, kindness, compassion, empathy, and how they interact with others. Having a healthy sense of self-worth will improve all relationships, especially the one with yourself (Ackerman, 2018).

We can all probably guess how a low sense of self-worth might look and feel but some may be unclear as to what healthy self-worth can look like. Below are three people with different skill levels who have a healthy sense of self-worth.

- Blair does not receive very good grades despite how much he studies and pays attention in class. He is a slow reader who often must reread passages to solidify understanding; his math skills are that of a toddler, and writing a letter is possibly the most difficult thing ever. Even though Blair isn't a stellar student, he still has a good sense of self-worth because he knows that grades and academic performance are not everything and do not define him. Blair knows he has many great qualities and abilities that make him worthy of love and respect (Ackerman, 2018).
- Romey likes to do a wide variety of things. He joined the local basketball and soccer leagues for adults. He rarely scores points in either sport and is often benched, but he shows up every week eager to play and interact with his teammates. Romey often volunteers to lead team meetings at work even though he often loses his train of thought and sometimes stutters. He also takes a cooking class once a week where he inevitably sets off the fire alarm. Romey knows that he is not the best at everything and accepts that making mistakes is part of life. Whether he spends the whole game on the bench, gets laughed at during a team meeting, or burns whatever he's trying to cook, Romey knows that he is still worthy of kindness, fun, love, and fulfillment.
- Emma is a very kind and dedicated person. She volunteers on weekends at a soup kitchen, and it is her job to prepare meals. Though many complain that her cooking leaves nothing to be desired, she still shows up and people are happy to see her

because she brings a positive energy into the space that makes up for her lack of cooking skills. She is an excellent salesperson and others look up to her, but there is always a coworker who is a step above. Even though Emma is not a great cook or the top employee at her job, she's okay with that and it doesn't change how she views herself: as someone worthy of love .

Just as Blair, Romey, and Emma demonstrate, you don't have to let your negative experiences define you or cause you to stop doing what you enjoy. Similarly, you do not have to let the love or lack of love others show you define your worth either. Just because it didn't work out between you and a lover, family member, friend, or coworker, doesn't mean that you are unlovable or that anything is wrong with you, it only reflects the incompatibility of your personalities and their inability to see your worth; that shows you who they are, not who you are. This is natural for everyone and the only way to move on is to know and accept that not everyone is going to like you, but that doesn't mean you are unlikeable. With that said, pick a hobby or something you enjoy and go do it regardless of your skill level. Do something that makes you feel happy and free without focusing on the outcome or final product; do so because you know that nothing can change your worth (Ackerman, 2018).

With this information along with the added introspection practices, you can begin to view healthy traits in other people and in yourself. It is possible that your toxic relationship and/or grief has isolated you from trusted loved ones. Reach out to friends or family whom you perceive as having a good sense of self-worth and try to rekindle that relationship. Chances are they are going to be happy to hear from you, relieved to know you are no longer spending time with someone who hurts you, and they will be glad to meet up and start hanging out again. It is scary to admit we need help or that we've gone through a tough time, but those who truly love us see our worth even when we don't. Spending time with them can help raise your sense of self-worth, and break you free from self-isolation (Sarkis, 2022).

**Breaking the Cycle**

Though you are going through a difficult time right now, you are able to channel this new knowledge of self and relationships into something useful. Not only can you help yourself next time, and toxic people are all around us so there is likely to be a next time, but you will be able to see red flags much sooner and make choices to protect your heart. You can use this newfound clarity to help others who you see struggling by sharing your story. Many people who go through breakups or end relationships with friends and family often feel that they are alone, that there is something wrong with them, or that they brought this on themselves. There will always be multiple perspectives to a story as we each experience the world through our own eyes; it is important to remember that just because the other person retells your experience to make themselves look like the victim, it does not invalidate what you went through. Feelings are feelings no matter if other people understand them or not.

If you think someone you know may be in a toxic relationship, talk to them about it. Like you, they may try to make excuses for the other person's behavior by explaining it away or telling you it's not that bad and they're just having a bad day, but you know from experience that this is not the case and you can help your friend by showing them that you care and checking in frequently. Them ending or staying in the relationship is not up to you, it is up to them and it is important that your friend knows they can come to you without fear of judgment. While they share their struggles with you, opportunities may arise for you to share as well. Without taking the focus off of their current situation, you could gently mention some traits that you may have overlooked in your past relationships; this may help your friend feel comfortable sharing more details with you (Spunout, 2021).

Toxic relationships beat us down and make us feel small and insignificant, when discussing the topic with your friend don't criticize them. They already feel bad enough without you adding to that, so instead try to build them up and remind them how wonderful they are. People with low self-worth often do not take compliments well, they'll brush them off, ignore them, or immediately compliment you to take the focus off of them (Spunout, 2021). In this case, you are kind of like a mentor. A mentor is someone with experience and knowledge on a topic or task that can serve as a guide to someone learning the same thing. For example, if you are starting a new job, you will likely have a mentor to train you; someone who has been there a while and knows the ins and outs of the company. A mentor for someone struggling with their mental health could be a psychologist, counselor, therapist, or you! We all learn from experience and from each other; you can mentor your friend by sharing your point-of-view, coaching them on self-love practices like journaling, meditation, or picking up a new hobby together. By helping your friend see what is great in them, they may begin to see it as well (Bencsik et al., 2014).

Just as you likely needed, your friend needs someone to vent to, someone to ask questions, to challenge what their partner, family, or friend has said about them to make them doubt themselves. It is important that you remain calm and not interrupt your friend; this is difficult because you love them and likely feel angry that someone is hurting them, but refrain from interrupting so they can get it all out. Sometimes, hearing it outloud or repeated back to them may trigger something inside that reminds them of who they are and that this behavior is not okay. You can gently suggest some websites, books, blogs, or therapists that were helpful for you and maybe beginning the research will help your friend make choices to protect their emotional and physical health. If your friend is not yet ready to open up about their relationship dilemma, or if they do not return phone calls or texts, don't stop calling or messaging. Your friend needs to know that they are not alone and that, no matter how much time passes, you are going to be there for them. Once they choose to open up, it is likely they will ask your opinion and it is important that you be direct and honest without judging their choices. Provide some concrete examples of what you have noticed to be unhealthy signs and share some tips for what has helped you (Spunout, 2021).

You can remind yourself and your friend that a growth mindset will help them to move through this pain and come out on the other side stronger and more confident. A growth mindset is one where we acknowledge our limitations but do not let those limitations stop us from trying, whereas a fixed mindset keeps us down and makes it difficult or even impossible to rise up. For example, in the beginning of a breakup, people often have a very fixed mindset where they tell themselves they will never feel happy again, that they are the problem to be fixed, that this is the biggest loss of their life. A growth mindset is when we let ourselves feel whatever emotions arise, but we know that this is temporary and we will try again when we are ready. The keyword to add to our dialogue is "yet." *I can't shake this feeling of sadness, yet, but I know it will get better. I can't ride a bike yet, but if I practice, I will learn.* Very simple, but highly effective in changing that inner voice who guides our emotions and thoughts (David, 2021).

Curiosity, kindness, and compassion can go a long way in bringing you or your friend out of difficult situations. Curious about what is to come now that that chapter in their lives is coming to an end? Kindness toward ourselves to know that this does not define our worth, compassion for others as we move through life together, facing challenges with an open-mind knowing that no matter what happens, and our worthiness of love and respect remains unchanged (David, 2021).

# Conclusion

There are so many wonderful things to be experienced in this life and I am proud of you for recognizing a problem and doing something about it. Throughout this book, you have perhaps learned where your idea of love and healthy relationships come from. In this, you can feel relieved that you are not at fault for the things you have gone through, but that you were using the tools you had to the best of your ability. Now, you can begin to make connections to current states of mind and outlooks on life with a new lens, you can notice what is real and what is not, and you have control over what enters and exists your life. You are stronger than you were before and you will get through whatever is hurting you.

Discovering toxicity around you is not pleasant and with this heightened awareness you may notice that you accept more than you should. Do not let this realization discourage you because there are loads of kind people for you to meet and build relationships with. You can now work on figuring out what you truly want in life, what you want out of your relationships and friendships, and what love should feel like. You are equipped with everything you need to learn your limitations and your strengths, you now know how to set boundaries. Setting boundaries and sticking to them are very different things; stay strong in knowing who you are and what you deserve because this will attract the right people into your life and reveal quickly the people who are undeserving of a place in your circle.

You make your life what you want it to be, and there are no set rules besides paying your bills on time, so, with this in mind, what kind of life are you going to create for yourself? What makes you happy and brings you joy? What do you love to do? Who brings you excitement and respect? Do more of what makes you happy and the rest of your life will likely follow, and when times arise where you feel defeated or like nothing is working out, remember your support system and know that you are not alone. It is human nature to go through ups and downs, to be unsure, to make mistakes, but it is through this that we learn, grow, evolve into brighter, conscious people. Working on ourselves is a time-consuming task that is in constant fluctuation as we move through life, and the more present we can manage to be moment-to-moment will enable us to react to situations with love and respect for ourselves and others. The human experience, while different for everyone, contains a huge range of emotions that guide our behavior. With the knowledge you have gained, it is hoped that you can view others and, especially yourself, with compassion and understanding. Not everyone deserves to be in your world, and you have the power to decide who and what you will invite in.

# REFERENCES

Ackerman, C. (2018, November 6). *What is Self-Worth and How Do We Increase it? (Incl. 4 Worksheets)*. PositivePsychology.

Arabi, S. (2018, August 9). *Why Narcissists Hoover And Remain Friends With Exes*. Psych Central. https://psychcentral.com/blog/recovering-narcissist/2018/08/research-finds-that-narcissists-try-to-remain-friends-with-their-exes-for-darker-reasons#4

Arene, C. (2021, December 22). *The Impact of Being in an Unhealthy Relationship* |.HealthyPlace.com. https://www.healthyplace.com/relationships/unhealthy-relationships/the-impact-of-being-in-an-unhealthy-relationship

Barhum, L. (2020, December 9). *Serious Ways Toxic Relationships Can Do Damage To Your Body*. HealthDigest.com. https://www.healthdigest.com/292616/serious-ways-toxic-relationships-can-do-damage-to-your-body/

Beheshti, N. (2020, May 15). *Toxic Influence: An Average Of 80% Of Americans Have Experienced Emotional Abuse*. Forbes. https://www.forbes.com/sites/nazbeheshti/2020/05/15/an-average-of-80-of-americans-have-experienced-emotional-abuse/?sh=7f28a0307b49

Bencsik, A., Juhász, T., & Machova, R. (2014). *Mentoring Practice on Behalf of Knowledge Sharing in the light of Education.* http://acta.uni-obuda.hu/Bencsik_Juhasz_Machova_55.pdf

Beuley Hunt, G. (2017, May 19). *How to Set Boundaries with a Toxic Friend*. PureWow. https://www.purewow.com/wellness/how-to-deal-with-toxic-friends

Brooten-Brooks, M. C. (2022, January 24). *How to Set Healthy Boundaries with Anyone*. Verywell Health. https://www.verywellhealth.com/setting-boundaries-5208802#toc-frequently-asked-questions-2e44502b-81c3-4ef9-990a-d34aaca4fbae

Career Contessa. (n.d.). *How to Establish Healthy Boundaries at Work*. Career Contessa. https://www.careercontessa.com/advice/healthy-boundaries-at-work/

Cherry, K. (2014, January 6). *A Look at Introspection*. Verywell Mind; Verywellmind. https://www.verywellmind.com/what-is-introspection-2795252

Cope, M. A., & Mattingly, B. A. (2020). Putting me back together by getting back together: Post-dissolution self-concept confusion predicts rekindling desire among anxiously attached individuals. *Journal of Social and Personal Relationships*, *38*(1), 384–392. Sage Journals. https://doi.org/10.1177/0265407520962849

David. (2021, July 29). *How to Make Friends & Meet New People - Meaningful Paths*. Meaningful Paths. https://www.meaningfulpaths.com/2021/07/29/how-to-make-friends-meet-new-people/

Davis, T. (n.d.). *Introspection: Definition (in Psychology), Examples, and Questions*. The Berkeley Well-Being Institute. https://www.berkeleywellbeing.com/introspection.html

Eatough, E. (2021, July 30). *Setting Boundaries in Relationships: A How-To*. Www.betterup.com. https://www.betterup.com/blog/setting-boundaries

Emamzadeh, A. (2022, January 10). *How to Increase Self-Motivation | Psychology Today*. Psychology Today. https://www.psychologytoday.com/us/blog/finding-new-home/202201/how-increase-self-motivation

Engel, B. (2002). *The emotionally abusive relationship: How to stop being abused and how to stop abusing*. John Wiley & Sons, Inc.

Everly, G. S. (2019, November 3). *Toxic People: How to Recognize and Avoid Them*. Psychology Today. https://www.psychologytoday.com/us/blog/when-disaster-strikes-inside-disaster-psychology/201911/toxic-people-how-recognize-and-avoid

Faitakis, M. (2021, January 1). *The Importance of Setting Boundaries*. The SMU Journal; Saint Mary's University's Independent Student Publication. https://www.thesmujournal.ca/editor/the-importance-of-setting-boundaries

Fazey, I., Fazey, J. A., & Fazey, D. M. A. (2005). Learning More Effectively from Experience. *Ecology and Society*, *10*(2). https://doi.org/10.5751/es-01384-100204

Gillis, K. (2022, July 1). *6 Steps Toward Recovery From a Toxic Relationship | Psychology Today*. Www.psychologytoday.com. https://www.psychologytoday.com/us/blog/invisible-bruises/202207/6-steps-toward-recovery-toxic-relationship

Glass, L. (1995). *Toxic people: 10 ways of dealing with people who make your life miserable.* Your Total Image Publishing. https://www.drlillianglass.com/wp-content/uploads/2015/06/Toxic-People_ebook.pdf

Gupta, S. (2021, January 2). *Here's how you can cut off toxic friends from your life, without stirring drama.* Healthshots. https://www.healthshots.com/mind/emotional-health/heres-how-you-can-cut-off-toxic-friends-from-your-life-without-stirring-drama/

Harbinger, J. (2022, April 25). *8 Signs It's Time to Cut a Toxic Person Out of Your Life (And How to Do It).* Jordan Harbinger. https://www.jordanharbinger.com/8-signs-its-time-to-cut-a-toxic-person-out-of-your-life-and-how-to-do-it/

Hood, J. (2020, February 3). *The benefits and importance of a support system | Highland Springs Clinic.* Highland Springs. https://highlandspringsclinic.org/the-benefits-and-importance-of-a-support-system/

Indeed Editorial Team. (2021, August 4). *16 Ways To Set Healthy Boundaries at Work.* Indeed Career Guide; Indeed.com. https://www.indeed.com/career-advice/career-development/boundaries-at-work

Johnson, E. B. (2020, June 1). *This is why you keep going back to the same toxic relationship.* Practical Growth. https://medium.com/practical-growth/why-you-keep-going-back-to-toxic-relationships-94d7e3a1d55b

Kane, A. (2022, March 10). *5 Steps to Setting Boundaries With Toxic Family Members | Better Humans.* Medium; Better Humans. https://betterhumans.pub/5-steps-to-setting-boundaries-with-toxic-family-members-1b3a87ec4b5b

Karakurt, G., & Silver, K. E. (2013). Emotional abuse in intimate relationships: The role of gender and age. *Violence and Victims*, *28*(5), 804–821. https://doi.org/10.1891/0886-6708.vv-d-12-00041

Koza, J. (2017, May 23). *5 Signs of Emotional Abuse*. Safe Horizon. https://www.safehorizon.org/programs/5-signs-emotional-abuse/

Lamonthe, C. (2022, January 11). *What Is a Toxic Relationship? 14 Signs and What to Do*. Healthline. https://www.healthline.com/health/toxic-relationship#leaving-a-toxic-relationship

Lamoreux, K. (2021, July 22). *Just Make It Stop! 10 Steps to End a Toxic Relationship*. Psych Central. https://psychcentral.com/blog/steps-to-end-a-toxic-relationship#log-emotions

Leonard, J. (2021, March 4). *How to let go of the past: Tips for relationships, regret, and trauma*. Www.medicalnewstoday.com. https://www.medicalnewstoday.com/articles/how-to-let-go-of-the-past#control

LifeStance Health. (2022, February 3). *The 4 Types of Trauma Responses*. LifeStance Health. https://lifestance.com/blog/four-types-trauma-response/

Martin, A., & Berenson, K. R. (2000). The Process of Leaving an Abusive Relationship: The Role of Risk Assessments and Decision Certainty. *The Journal of Family Violence*, *15*(2), 109–122. ResearchGate. https://doi.org/10.1023/A:1007515514298

Martin, S. (2019a, October 17). *Cutting Ties with Toxic Family Members: An Act of Self-Care*. Live Well with Sharon Martin. https://www.livewellwithsharonmartin.com/cutting-ties-with-toxic-family/

Martin, S. (2019b, October 18). *Its Okay to Cut Ties with Toxic Family Members*. Psych Central. https://psychcentral.com/blog/imperfect/2019/10/its-okay-to-cut-ties-with-toxic-family-members#5-Reasons-we-struggle-to-cut-ties-with-a-toxic-family-member

Martin, S. (2020, April 30). *How to Set Boundaries with Toxic People*. Psych Central. https://psychcentral.com/blog/imperfect/2020/04/how-to-set-boundaries-with-toxic-people#Learn-more

Mayo Clinic. (2017, November 18). *Narcissistic personality disorder - Symptoms and causes*. Mayo Clinic. https://www.mayoclinic.org/diseases-conditions/narcissistic-personality-disorder/symptoms-causes/syc-20366662#:~:text=Overview

Merinuk, M. (2022, February 18). *Are you in a toxic friendship? How to spot the signs*. TODAY.com. https://www.today.com/health/behavior/toxic-friendship-warning-signs-rcna16665

Moss, J. (2021, December 26). *How to recognize a toxic workplace and what to do about it: Jennifer Moss*. CBC. https://www.cbc.ca/news/canada/kitchener-waterloo/jennifer-moss-toxic-work-environment-1.6289475

Pace, R. (2022, May 19). *Cutting People Off: When It's the Right Time and How to Do It*. Marriage Advice - Expert Marriage Tips & Advice. https://www.marriage.com/advice/relationship/cutting-people-off/#When_should_you_cut_someone_out_of_your_life

Pai, D. (2018). *The negative health effects of a bad relationship*. Quora; Keck School of Medicine at University of South California (USC). https://www.quora.com/Are-there-negative-health-effects-when-it-comes-to-bad-relationships/answer/Keck-Medicine-of-USC

Perna, M. C. (2022, June 1). *Toxic Work Culture Is The #1 Factor Driving People To Resign*. Forbes. https://www.forbes.com/sites/markcperna/2022/06/01/toxic-work-culture-is-the-1-factor-driving-people-to-resign/?sh=5cf9fa2768f1

Radin, S. (2020, September 14). *The Emotional Aftermath of Cutting Ties With a Toxic Family Member*. Allure. https://www.allure.com/story/cutting-off-toxic-family-member

Sarkis, S. A. (2022, June 28). *How to Recover From a Toxic Relationship | Psychology Today*. Www.psychologytoday.com. https://www.psychologytoday.com/intl/blog/here-there-and-everywhere/202206/how-recover-toxic-relationship

Seidman, G. (2016, September 16). *What's Really Going on When People Stay in Touch With Exes | Psychology Today*. Psychology Today. https://www.psychologytoday.com/us/blog/close-encounters/201609/whats-really-going-when-people-stay-in-touch-exes

Sells, S. (2019, January 10). *Why Do We Go Back To Toxic Relationships? A Sexologist Explains*. HelloGiggles. https://hellogiggles.com/love-sex/relationships/why-do-we-go-back-to-people-who-hurt-us-sexologist/

Selva, J. (2018, January 5). *How to Set Healthy Boundaries: 10 Examples + PDF Worksheets*. PositivePsychology.com. https://positivepsychology.com/great-self-care-setting-healthy-boundaries/

Solferino, N., & Tessitore, M. E. (2019, July 30). *Human Networks and Toxic Relationships*. ResearchGate. https://www.researchgate.net/publication/335444973_Human_networks_and_toxic_relationships

Spunout. (2021). *How can I help someone in a toxic relationship?* SpunOut.ie - Ireland's Youth Information Website. https://spunout.ie/sex-relationships/relationships/help-someone-toxic-relationship

Steber, C. (2019, March 2). *7 Reasons Why It's So Difficult To Leave An Unhealthy Relationship*. Bustle. https://www.bustle.com/p/7-reasons-why-its-so-difficult-to-leave-unhealthy-relationship-16003317#:~:text=But%20when%20it%20comes%20to

Sull, D., Sull, C., & Zweig, B. (2022, January 11). *Toxic Culture Is Driving the Great Resignation*. MIT Sloan Management Review. https://sloanreview.mit.edu/article/toxic-culture-is-driving-the-great-resignation/

Taub, A. (2020, April 6). A New Covid-19 Crisis: Domestic Abuse Rises Worldwide. *The New York Times*. https://www.nytimes.com/2020/04/06/world/coronavirus-domestic-violence.html

Taylor Counseling Group. (2022, March 3). *10 Ways To Set Boundaries With Difficult Family Members*. Taylor Counseling Group. https://taylorcounselinggroup.com/blog/set-boundaries-for-difficult-family-members/

Thompson, R. (2021, October 14). *Jonah Hill sets boundary with followers, asks them not to comment on his body*. Mashable. https://mashable.com/article/jonah-hill-boundary-comments-about-body

Vincenty, S. (2021, October 6). *Is Your Family Toxic?* Oprah Daily. https://www.oprahdaily.com/life/relationships-love/a29609819/signs-of-toxic-family/

Zarrabi, R. (2022, March 9). *11 Reasons Why People Don't Let Go of Unhealthy Relationships | PsychologyToday*. Www.psychologytoday.com. https://www.psychologytoday.com/us/blog/mindful-dating/202203/11-reasons-why-people-dont-let-go-unhealthy-relationships

Made in United States
North Haven, CT
30 May 2023

37158060R00065